PRAISE FOR *THE BEAUTY OF INTOLERANCE*

"Here's a timely message—clearly presented, creatively explained, effectively argued, and lovingly offered as an antidote to the confusion so many people feel about this vital topic."

—Lee Strobel, bestselling author and professor,
Houston Baptist University

"There is incredible confusion over the nature of tolerance. Should we be tolerant? Intolerant? The McDowells provide valuable insight, compelling stories, and practical steps for seeing through the cultural confusion so you can lovingly stand for truth."

—David Limbaugh, lawyer and author of *The Emmaus Code*

"*The Beauty of Intolerance* is perhaps the most needed book in the library of lives around the world second only to the Bible. Unlike some teaching, preaching, and cults, all roads do not lead to heaven but actually to hell. We can coexist on Earth, but apart from the shed blood of Christ and repentance of sin, we will not coexist in heaven. Josh and Sean have penned a game-changer because they didn't change the Word. Yes, intolerance is beautiful but misleading the masses is beyond ugly. May millions read this book and fall in love with The Book [Bible]."

—Frank Shelton, author, Washington, DC field rep,
MY HOPE with Billy Graham & evangelist, Waldorf, MD

D01124339
W9-ASJ-212

THE BEAUTY OF
INTOLERANCE

Print ISBN 978-1-63058-940-0

eBook Editions:
Adobe Digital Edition (.epub) 978-1-63409-742-0
Kindle and MobiPocket Edition (.prc) 978-1-63409-743-7

Cover design: Faceout Studio, www.faceoutstudio.com

Published by Shiloh Run Press, an imprint of Barbour Publishing, Inc., P.O. Box 719, Uhrichsville, Ohio 44683, www.shilohrunpress.com.

Our mission is to publish and distribute inspirational products offering exceptional value and biblical encouragement to the masses.

 Member of the
Evangelical Christian
Publishers Association

Printed in the United States of America.

THE BEAUTY OF

INTOLERANCE

SETTING A GENERATION FREE TO KNOW
TRUTH & LOVE

JOSH MCDOWELL
SEAN MCDOWELL

SHILOH RUN PRESS
An Imprint of Barbour Publishing, Inc.

DEDICATION

Dad, thanks for not only defending truth
but also for modeling what it means to
love those with whom we significantly
disagree. You taught me true tolerance in
your actions and your words.
—SEAN

ACKNOWLEDGMENTS

We wish to recognize the following individuals for their valuable contribution to this book.

Troy Peiffer, for all the valuable research he provided to us on this project.

Matthew Anderson, Jason Carlson, and Amy Hall, for reviewing the manuscript and providing valuable insight. Each of you helped to significantly improve the quality and clarity of this book.

Tom Williams, for editing the manuscript and applying his valuable insights, wordsmithing skills, and passionate heart to help make these words come alive on the printed page.

Don Kencke, for reviewing the manuscript and providing insightful guidance.

Amanda Price, for editing the manuscript to bring the book to completion.

And last but not least, we are grateful to the team at Barbour Publishing for having a vision for this project and partnering with us to make it a success.

Josh McDowell
Sean McDowell

CONTENTS

CHAPTER 1

TRUE FOR YOU
BUT NOT FOR ME

"You'll love him, Mom," Renee said energetically on her visit home from her second year in college. "He's so considerate, and he's smart and really good looking."

Teri smiled. "That's great, honey," she said. "What's he majoring in?"

"Business management, just like me."

"That's good. Does he have your same church background, too?"

"Mom," Renee responded with a tinge of irritation in her voice. "Let's not get into church stuff again."

"I'm not," Teri protested. "I just wanted to know if he shares our family's values, that's all."

"Tony doesn't go to church, okay?" Renee stated outright. "He's not an atheist or anything; he's just not into church and religious stuff."

"Who's not into religious stuff?" The voice was that of Renee's father, Kenton, who had just walked into the room.

"Renee was just telling me about her new friend, Tony," Teri replied. "She said he isn't into church."

"What is he, an atheist?" Kenton asked.

"Come on, you guys," Renee retorted, sounding even more irritated. "Tony's a great guy! Whether he goes to church or not isn't an issue with me."

"Well, it is with me," Kenton said firmly.

"Look, Dad," Renee began, "I don't want to get into this discussion right now, okay? Because Tony and I don't believe just like you guys, that doesn't make us bad."

"Honey, no one is saying you're bad," Teri responded, trying to temper the rising tension in the conversation. "What your dad and I want is for you to be happy and not get hurt, that's all. But"—she raised her hand like a policeman stopping traffic to silence Renee's inevitable retort—"let's move on. So when can we meet Tony, anyway?"

"Actually, we were hoping we could both come here for Christmas break—not for the entire two weeks, of course. We want to spend part of it with his parents, too. But at least long enough that you can get to know each other."

"That's a wonderful idea, honey. Your dad and I would love it. Just let us know ahead of time which days you'll be here, and I'll have the guest room ready."

Renee hesitated. "Sure, Mom. But—" She took a deep breath. "Well, like, is the guest room really necessary? I was thinking we could just stay in my room together."

Teri's eyes went wide with shock, but Kenton responded first. "Don't be silly. You can't do that. You know it's not right."

"I thought you'd say that," Renee responded. "I explained to Tony how you and Mom feel about that sort of thing, but I promised to talk to you about it anyway. I don't see why you can't just accept my lifestyle choices and me. But don't worry. We'll respect your feelings and sleep in separate rooms while we're here."

Teri's heart pounded like drums. "While you're here?" Her voice went high and shrill. "What do you mean 'while you're here'? Are you trying to tell us that you two intend to sleep together when you're not here?"

"We already do, Mom. We're in love. You don't really expect us to—"

Kenton interrupted. "I expect you to honor the morals and values your mother and I taught you all your life."

"I do," Renee countered. "That's why I agreed that we would sleep in separate rooms while we're here. But at Tony's house or at school, it's different."

Kenton tried to keep his composure. "Are you trying to tell me that Tony's parents have no problem with your sleeping together at their house?"

"No, Dad, they don't. After all, not everyone shares your views on that sort of thing, you know."

Kenton shook his head. "I know that," he said, trying to rein in his emotions. "But I certainly thought our daughter did share them."

Renee took a deep breath and spoke in a softer tone. "Dad, in many ways, I do share your views. You and Mom have taught me a lot. But there are some things I have to decide for myself. What you guys decided to do before you got married was your choice. I've made my choice, and I wish you guys could respect that and not judge me. In fact, I wish you could see that these choices are just as right for me as yours were for you."

Kenton shook his head slowly. Teri stifled a sob. "I love you, honey," she said. "I just don't see how you can so easily abandon the values we raised you with."

WHY THEY CAN'T AGREE

Renee's parents want her to do what's right. But as far as Renee is concerned, she *is* doing what's right. She acknowledges that her parents didn't live together before they got married because they believed it was wrong for them to do so. But Renee doesn't think those values apply to her because she has determined that living with a boy she is serious about is a wise way to go. In fact, having seen many of her friends' parents divorce, she likely believes it's a good step to ensure the best long-term relationship. She would like her parents to be tolerant by respecting and endorsing her decision. Since they don't, a conflict has become inevitable.

Are Renee's differing views from her parents' just part of the infamous generation gap? Differences separating adults from their children have always existed to some degree. I (Josh) have a different perspective on a number of issues from that of my grown son, Sean. And I (Sean) sometimes see life from a different point of view than that of my father. This may be considered somewhat of a generation gap, yet we are bound together through a common set of core values. Our shared beliefs and value system bridge whatever differing views we may have on various subjects, and they enable us to work closely together, as we are doing in coauthoring this book.

It's natural—and if done properly, even healthy—for the people of each new generation to establish a unique identity apart from their parents. Yet what we are experiencing today is far from the typical generation gap. We are seeing a cultural shift that is separating Christian parents from their children perhaps unlike anything seen before.

Renee is calling for her parents to be understanding. She wants her mom and dad to realize that she has the right to define sexual issues and marriage for herself. In fact, what she really desires is for her parents not only to respect her own brand of morality, but also to acknowledge that it isn't wrong for her to do what she personally feels is right. If her parents respond in any way short of that, she will consider them to be intolerant.

If you are like most Christian parents, grandparents, or gatekeepers of young people (pastors, youth pastors, Christian educators), you are no doubt perplexed by a new younger generation of teens and twentysomethings that seems comfortable with a value system and set of beliefs that are often contrary to biblical standards. It's not that you don't want to be understanding of another person's view—especially if it's your own child—but you don't want to endorse what you feel is biblically wrong either. Yet most of this generation doesn't consider what they believe or how they behave to be wrong. In fact, they think their moral views are correct for them. They have adopted a different moral compass for evaluating truth, and so they often make radically different choices in the area of sex and relationships than those of their parents. This is the case with Renee.

Renee's parents are troubled, and rightly so. But what they don't seem to recognize is that Renee isn't entirely wrong. Yet neither is she entirely right. From Renee's point of view, failure to accept her moral choices amounts to a rejection not only of her beliefs but of her personally. She and an entire new younger generation are calling for more tolerance of a diverse culture. They want to be loved even though their beliefs and lifestyle may be different from those of previous generations. That is understandable. For youth to feel personally rejected when parents and friends are not accepting of what they do is natural.

As a former high school teacher, I (Sean) can tell you that many students have felt rejected and judged when their behavior or ideas differed from the behavior or ideas of their parents. It is not easy to disapprove of our children's behavior while at the same time making them feel loved as people of great worth. Oftentimes these two concepts seem to be in conflict with each other, and thus their relationship to each other is not clearly understood. Consequently, young people feel rejected, and distance forms between them and their parents.

Two very different understandings of tolerance are at odds here. Renee and most of her generation are in effect saying, "Be tolerant of me—which includes accepting my views and acknowledging that my behavior is right for me." Many Christian adults respond with, "I'll be glad to be tolerant by accepting you and giving you the freedom to live your own life, but don't ask me to approve of your behavior or consider it to be right." These are two differing views on tolerance, and they are creating a cultural chasm that is almost impossible to bridge without first understanding the real nature of moral truth. What we find today is that most young people have adopted a different source of moral truth than that of their parents and Christian gatekeepers. And these two different sources create different narratives about reality that frame each side's view on tolerance, moral values, and relationships differently—including how we are to accept and love others.

Our point in including fictional stories in this book is not to take sides with either the parents or their children. We agree and disagree with various aspects of how *each* of them respond. We want to highlight how these conversations often go and draw some generalizations about how two differing generations tend to view tolerance. As you will see through the progression of the book, we believe it is possible to truly love and accept people with whom we significantly disagree. This is the path Jesus took. And it is the one we are called to today—even if such an approach is increasingly considered intolerant.

DIFFERENT SOURCE OF TRUTH

Truth, specifically moral truth, lays the foundation for how we understand and express such ideas as tolerance, respect, dignity, acceptance, moral judgments, and a host of other attitudes. No doubt you have already discovered that today's young adult generation largely holds to a different source of moral truth than you do. The majority of young people—even in your church and perhaps in your own home—accept a different narrative on how moral truth plays out in our lives. And that makes a world of difference in how to communicate with and understand today's youth.

Your narrative about truth is probably based on your understanding of the Bible. Whether they realize it or not, our young people today largely derive their narrative about truth from a culture that says moral truth is found within the individual. These two narratives can be expressed in terms of the *biblical narrative about truth* and the *cultural narrative about truth*. When our young people accept the cultural narrative, it becomes the lens by which they interpret relationships and much of the world around them. These two narratives can be stated in this way:

- *The biblical narrative:* Moral truth is grounded in the character of God; it is objective and universal. This truth is known by discovering the nature of God and his ways as revealed through scripture and within nature.
- *The cultural narrative:* Moral truth comes from the individual; it is subjective and situational. This truth is known through choosing to believe it and through personal experience (i.e., you are the creator of your own truth).

Renee, in our story, has clearly looked to the culture for her understanding of truth. Unwittingly, most of our young people today have done the same. They are probably unaware of how the culture has so deeply shaped their view of truth. So it is understandable that a new generation would define sexual morality differently than their parents or scripture. Renee believes she has the right to determine for herself whether living with her boyfriend is right or wrong for her. Her parents might say that she has "the right" to *choose for herself*, too. Yet they disagree on how to exercise that right and believe that God and his Word have already determined that what she is doing is wrong, and it isn't up for negotiation. With these two opposing perspectives on the source of morality, you can understand how communication and mutual understanding would be hampered. The reality is, most of our young people are using many of the same words as we do to define moral truth, but those words have taken on a different meaning for them. And we simply can't come to an understanding with another person when words and terms don't mean the same for each party involved.

Some time ago a youth worker shared that he was recognizing how the young people in his group understood words differently than he did. He put it this way: "I have ministered to my kids every week for a year now, and I've come to this conclusion: we use the same words as our young people, but they mean totally different things. Words like *tolerance, respect, acceptance, moral judgments*, and *personal preference* have a completely different meaning to my kids than they do to me. We were working from two different premises, and I didn't even know it. I'm convinced unless I can get my kids to rethink some basic Christian concepts, I'll never make it to square one with them."

This youth worker is confronting what many churches and families confront on a daily basis. Like him, many are unaware of the differing definitions their teens are applying to various words. Words like *tolerance, respect, dignity, acceptance, moral judgment*, and *personal preference* all have taken on different meanings due to the differing sources of moral truth young people have adopted. Consider some of the differences in the following chart:

Word	Biblical Understanding	Contemporary Cultural Understanding
Tolerance	Recognize and respect others when you don't share their values, beliefs, and practices.	Recognize and respect that every individual's values, truth claims, beliefs, and practices are equally valid.
Respect	Give due consideration to others as valuable human beings, without necessarily endorsing their beliefs and lifestyle choices.	Wholeheartedly approve of others' beliefs or lifestyle choices as equally valid.
Dignity	Created in the image of God, humans have an inherent and inalienable worth of infinite value.	Humans have an inherent worth shaped and realized by personal choice and standards created by the individual.[1]
Acceptance	Embrace people regardless of their beliefs and lifestyle choices.	Not only endorse, but actually praise others for their beliefs and lifestyle choices.
Moral Judgments	Certain things are morally right and wrong, as determined by God's Word.	No one has the right to judge another person's moral truth or behavior.
Personal Preference	Individual preferences of art, food, clothing style, hobbies, etc., are personally determined.	Individual preferences of sexual behaviors, value systems, and beliefs are personally determined.

THE INSEPARABLE NATURE OF TRUTH AND TOLERANCE

Of all the words on the chart on page 21, the one that most clearly represents today's cultural narrative of moral truth is the word *tolerance*. When individuals think of themselves as their own source for creating moral truth, it's only natural for them to feel no one has the right to judge whatever they choose to believe or do. Acceptance of them includes acceptance of their moral truth. After all, if each person is a valid, independent source of applied truth, then there can be no basis for external disapproval. There is no overarching standard by which to apply judgment. That means tolerance as the culture defines it is the only appropriate response to each individual's moral choices. That kind of tolerance—what we will call *cultural tolerance*—propagates the notion that all moral truth is equal. From that perspective it only seems right to respect, accept, and approve of diverse views and the behavior of others, since doing otherwise would be intolerant and judgmental.

I (Sean) have interacted with a lot of high school students from good Christian homes. They want to be accepting of others, and they resist the idea of judging people. They want to be tolerant because they want to treat people well. This is a good thing. But what many of today's young people don't understand is that they have unwittingly bought into cultural tolerance, which is a faulty narrative about moral truth that fundamentally changes the traditional meaning of words like *tolerance, acceptance, respect*, and the like. They tend to think that they have the right to determine what is right and wrong for themselves. They, like Renee, tend to confuse the difference between defining right and wrong for oneself and determining what is actually right and wrong. It is God's character that determines what is morally right and wrong, and it is his Word that reveals that truth to us.

God is not only the standard of what is true—he *is* truth—but he is also the perfect standard for tolerance. That is, he is the standard for tolerance in the original and traditional meaning of the word—a tolerance that loves us without approving of our sinful condition. Both truth and traditional tolerance reside in the character of God, and they are inseparable.

Authors and social ethics professors Dr. Brad Stetson and Dr. Joseph G. Conti explain the inseparable nature of truth and traditional tolerance this way: "[Traditional] tolerance gives to truth the cognitive freedom it needs to be authentically recognized, and truth gives to [traditional] tolerance the parameters and purpose it needs to function as it is intended—to serve people and communities in their quest for meaning and ultimately the knowledge of the One in whom alone lies their fulfillment."[2] In other words, truth and traditional tolerance are the necessary balancing ingredients to genuinely love and accept others unconditionally.

Understanding this dynamic empowers us to express an unconditional love and acceptance for another without necessarily approving of his or her behavior. Renee's parents and all of us want to be sure our children feel loved, even though at times we can't agree with their attitudes or actions. By understanding how truth and traditional tolerance work together, we unlock the key to making our children feel loved even when we can't approve of what they choose and what they do. It also gives us insight into how we can effectively counter the influence that cultural tolerance is having on our young people. In the pages that follow, we will discover together how to accomplish this.

WHEN INTOLERANCE IS BEAUTIFUL

As we have said, Renee and many in our culture today are asking for us to be culturally tolerant of behavior that is contrary to biblical commands and values. Cultural tolerance does not simply require that we give others the freedom to believe or live differently than we do. It has evolved into a demand that we accept, respect, and affirm the rightness of others' views and behavior—or be labeled intolerant, bigoted, and even hateful. Correcting this error of definition will require more than simply redefining the word *tolerance*. As we have indicated, ultimately the meaning of tolerance has changed within our culture because the source our young people look to for moral truth has changed.

But what many fail to realize may surprise you. Traditional tolerance is truly a virtue, and intolerance can sometimes be beautiful—that is, when you understand it from God's point of view. What is more virtuous than a holy God responding to sinful humanity through his tolerant expressions of love, acceptance, and mercy? What is more beautiful than God's intolerance expressed in his moral outrage toward the tragedies of poverty, racism, sexual abuse, slavery, AIDS, bigotry, and other such evils?

God is both our definer and our model for true tolerance and intolerance. Consider what happened when the first humans failed to trust God and rejected his offer of eternal life. Scripture tells us their sin and evil "broke his heart" (Genesis 6:6). It is understandable that a perfect and holy God could not have a relationship with sin. The Bible says of him, "Your eyes are too pure to look on evil; you cannot tolerate wrongdoing" (Habakkuk 1:13 NIV). Yet God is the pure expression of traditional tolerance and the perfect manifestation of love. He took on human nature (the Incarnation), accepted us in spite of our wrongdoing, and died as a sacrifice and payment for sin so we could be forgiven and ultimately live in relationship with him forever. Now that's being truly tolerant and loving!

While the Incarnation is the personification of love and acceptance, God's disdain for sin reflects his holy intolerance. What sin did to humans broke his heart. Separated from God, the human race wallowed in greed, lust, jealousy, hatred, and conflict. Human sin has rippled down from one generation to another with the same tragic results: pain and suffering, heartache and ruin, destruction and death. God's hatred of evil and injustice—of everything that hurts us—prompted him to be radically intolerant of sin and its devastating effects on his creation. His amazing love for us prompted him to do something to save us from it. That something cost him the death of his only Son, but he considered you and me worth it. God's intolerance is an amazing and beautiful thing.

I (Josh) was struck by this beautiful nature of intolerance and came up with an idea that placed intolerance in its proper context. I created a T-shirt. On the front it says, "Intolerance is a Beautiful Idea." On the back it reads:

Mother Teresa was intolerant of poverty.
Bono was intolerant of AIDS.
Nelson Mandela was intolerant of apartheid.
Martin Luther King was intolerant of racism.
Jesus was intolerant of bigotry.

As you can imagine, I've had a lot of people respond to it—almost 100 percent positively. Why? Because universally people tend to accept the moral truth that poverty, AIDS, apartheid, racism, and bigotry are wrong and should not be tolerated. The point is, it is the biblical source of truth and its narrative that give tolerance and intolerance their proper definition and understanding. When we are able to understand this biblical narrative of truth and pass that on to our children, it allows them to embrace God's perspective on tolerance, intolerance, love, sexual morality, and our overall purpose and meaning for life. While it is true that most young people are not embracing the biblical narrative of truth and are reaping negative consequences, we have reason for hope.

THE TRUTH WILL SET THEM FREE

The good news is that our young people are still in the process of formulating their views on issues of tolerance and moral truth. Their views are by no means set in concrete and impossible to reverse, so there is still a window of opportunity to share why the biblical narrative of truth is right and far more beneficial to them and to the world on many levels. This is true not only for young people but for *anyone* embracing the false view of tolerance. And it is not difficult to show how adopting the culture's narrative of truth is ill-conceived, toxic, and unfulfilling. The cultural take on moral truth, and particularly the idea of tolerance, may on the surface appear extremely virtuous and genuinely good. It feels like the most caring option. It seems so accepting of others and nonjudgmental. But when we contrast the cultural narrative of truth with the biblical narrative of truth, we can see that cultural tolerance does not actually show respect for others or even demonstrate care for them—it does the opposite.

So, together in the chapters that follow, we will unpack our contemporary culture's idea of tolerance and the contrasting biblical narrative of moral truth. We will explain how the differing views on moral truth relate to sexual choices, ethical standards and values, our view of God, our view of ourselves, acceptance of others, and loving relationships. Step by step we will discover how biblical truth actually peels back the curtain to expose the error of the cultural view and its champion—tolerance. We will demonstrate how damaging the cultural view of tolerance is to the individual and to relationships. We will go on to explain how you can lead your youth to a biblical narrative of truth that will show them what true respect, love, and acceptance look like. You can help lead your children to understand who defines morality and what determines right from wrong. When you and your young people know the real source of truth, you will experience clarity, compassion, and conviction. You will be enabled to discern what is true and what is error. Jesus said that when you "know the truth. . .the truth will set you free" (John 8:32). That is, only when we know right and wrong will we realize our own sin and need for repentance, come to see the truth about what Jesus has done for us, and believe. We are only truly set free when we embrace and live the message of Jesus.

WHY THERE IS SUCH HOPE

This generation of young people exemplified by Renee is calling for tolerance of practically every belief and lifestyle under the sun. And their call for a new kind of tolerance is increasingly influencing older generations as well. Renee and the rest of her generation want to make decisions and choices on their own and still be accepted. Today's young people rightly want others to see them for who they are—warts and all—and love what they see. We all want that. They call for a new tolerance in hopes of being celebrated for their uniqueness—those things that set them apart. They want to be validated for who they are and what they feel. Yet what they want, and in fact need, can never be attained by the kind of tolerance they have adopted—the tolerance defined by today's culture.

As bad as it may sometimes seem and as fearful as you may be that your children have been negatively influenced by the culture around them—there is hope. It's true that cultural tolerance is almost everywhere. Your children are inundated with its teachings in the educational system, the government, the arts, the media, even within the church. But as a parent you are still a powerful influence in your children's lives.

Consider this: a national online study shows that 45 percent of young people consider their parents to be their role models.[3] Perhaps you thought today's musical icon or young movie stars or sports celebrities were your childrens' role models. But they are not. Another study shows that 32 percent of today's young people look to their friends and just 15 percent look to celebrities for guidance and inspiration.[4] In fact, yet another study shows that until a child reaches twenty-five years of age, the greatest influence on that child's behavior will be the loving, close relationship with his or her parents, particularly that of the father.[5] Researchers at the University of Florida recently stated that "the good news is that most teens *are* listening to what parents are saying despite what they [the parents] think."[6]

We live in an exciting age. God is not taken off guard by the loss of morals in society or the rejection of his universal truths by virtually an entire culture. He is at work in your community, in your ministry, and in your home to make his light of truth penetrate the cultural fog and reach your children. As the apostle Paul said, "If God is for us, who can ever be against us?" (Romans 8:31).

Sadly, there are people in places of influence who are fierce proponents of the doctrine of today's tolerance, and this makes your task more difficult. But your primary fight is not with people as you are "destroy[ing] every proud obstacle that keeps people from knowing God" (2 Corinthians 10:5). Paul said, "We are not fighting against flesh-and-blood enemies, but against evil rulers and authorities of the unseen world" (Ephesians 6:12). This is a spiritual struggle for the hearts and minds of your young people, and we want to help you win. Through God's Word and the empowerment of the Holy Spirit, you have a golden opportunity to lead your young people to embrace a value system based on God and his Word. Because we truly believe that, we have written this book. With God's help you can raise up the next generation to live as "children of God without fault in a warped and crooked generation," in which they "shine. . .like stars in the sky" (Philippians 2:15 NIV). Let's do it!

CHAPTER 2

WHEN TOLERANCE DOESN'T MEAN TOLERANCE

"We're out of here," seventeen-year-old Chad called out to his dad as he and his friend Mike headed toward the door.

"Where you going so fast?" Todd asked.

"The GG9 is having its track and field this afternoon," Chad replied. "So Mike and I are going to watch."

"The GG what?" Todd inquired.

"Dad, it's been all over the news. Aren't you up on it?"

"Up on what? I don't know what you're talking about."

"Mr. Arnold," Mike responded, "the GG9 is the international Gay Games, something like the Olympics, that happens every four years. And this year part of it is in our city. My older brother is running in the relay race today."

"Ohhhhh, those games. Yeah, I have been reading some about them, and, uh, I'm not really comfortable with you going, son." Todd looked straight at Chad.

"Okay, you're not comfortable, so I'm not asking you to go," Chad retorted. "But I'm comfortable going, and we've made big plans to take in the relay race. It doesn't cost anything to get in."

"Well, I'm sorry you've made plans. I'm just saying my son is not going to any gay games, and that's that," Todd stated emphatically.

"Why not?" Chad shot back. "What's the big deal?"

"Look," Todd began, leaning forward in his chair, "I don't have anything against those people personally. I just don't like them pushing their lifestyle on the rest of society with games just for them and all their gay rights agenda and everything."

"Stop it, Dad!"

"I know you boys don't like to hear this," Todd continued. "But there comes a time to stand up for what's right and decent. Homosexuality is wrong, and we shouldn't be celebrating it, for crying out loud!"

"I'm out of here," Mike said as he turned to Chad. "Text me when you get a chance." As Mike made his way out the door, Chad turned toward his father.

"I can't believe you," Chad said, his dark gaze bewildered and accusing.

"Hey, I'm just trying to help you take a stand here, Chad."

"Take a stand against my friends?"

"What are you talking about?"

"For one thing, Mike's brother is gay. His dad kicked him out of the house, and it's like you just kicked Mike out."

"Just slow down a minute here," Todd replied, raising his hand in protest. "First off, I didn't kick anyone out of our house. And second, until you mentioned the race, I didn't even know Mike's brother was gay."

"It doesn't matter, Dad. The way you're against gays is just so judgmental. If I do something that you really disagree with, are you going to kick me out of the house like Mike's father did? What if I said I was gay? You would probably disown me or something, wouldn't you?"

"Okay, settle down, Chad," Todd responded.

"No, I'm not going to settle down," Chad said defiantly. "Come on, admit that you hate gays. And if I was gay, you'd hate me, too, right?"

"That's ridiculous, Chad."

"It's not ridiculous!" Chad said as he turned toward the door. "I just can't believe you are full of such hate toward people who are different than you."

And with that Chad stalked out of the house, slamming the door behind him.

THE GREAT DIVIDE

We can see that a moral divide exists between Chad and his father as well as between Renee and her parents from chapter 1. Perhaps there is no greater issue today that illustrates that divide than homosexuality. The current culture, including many young people from Christian homes, claims that conservative Christians hate gays, discriminate against them, and are overall intolerant bigots.

Researchers and authors David Kinnaman and Gabe Lyons make this pointed statement in their book *unChristian: What a New Generation Really Thinks about Christianity. . .and Why It Matters*: "When you introduce yourself as a Christian to a friend, neighbor, or business associate who is an outsider, you might as well have it tattooed on your arm: anti-homosexual, gay-hater, homophobic."[1] While that obviously isn't an accurate reflection of most Christian attitudes toward gay people, the majority of young Americans, up to 90 percent, tend to think "anti-homosexual" describes present-day Christians.[2]

This biased belief that leads people to think Christians discriminate against gay people has certainly been perpetuated by groups that call themselves Christian yet act unchristian. There are those wearing the label of Christianity who have denounced the gay community with hateful language and stood on street corners wielding signs proclaiming, GOD HATES FAGS. Of course those views and actions don't represent the majority of Christians in America. In fact, those views represent a tiny minority. Yet they have created a hypersensitivity that causes certain groups and local city officials to sniff out discrimination even where it doesn't exist.

For example, the city of Coeur d'Alene, Idaho, threatened to arrest two Christian ministers who refused to perform same-sex weddings. According to a lawsuit filed in federal court, the ministers were told they had to "either perform same-sex weddings or face jail time and up to a $1,000 fine."[3] This Idaho city and its city council obviously thought the two ministers discriminated against gays because they believed marriage should be between a man and a woman and acted on that belief.

The Christian community, on the other hand, often counter-charges that they are being denied their right of free speech when it comes to voicing their conviction on same-sex marriage. When John McAdams, associate professor at Marquette University in Milwaukee, Wisconsin, let it be known where he stood, he was suspended. McAdams's offense was that he criticized a fellow teacher who had prevented a student from discussing his opposing view of gay rights in the instructor's Theory of Ethics class. The teacher told the student after class that "any opposition to same-sex marriage is to be considered offensive speech and will not be tolerated in her class."[4] Professor McAdams blogged his disapproval of the teacher's stifling a student's free expression of belief and was quickly suspended and banned from the campus while his actions were under investigation. The teacher was allowed to criticize the student to the point of banning his speech, but McAdams was denied the right to criticize the teacher for doing so.

Such is the culture we live in today. Freedom of speech and freedom of religion seem to be protected rights until one crosses the line in opposition to same-sex marriage and homosexual behavior.

This book is not primarily about the fallacies of same-sex marriage or a defense for God's design for marriage. Homosexuality and the gay movement, however, serve as an ideal example of how we as a Christian community are divided from the culture when it comes to: (1) what it means to be tolerant and intolerant; (2) who or what is to judge what is morally right and wrong; (3) what it means to accept without approving; (4) how we are to demonstrate proper respect and care for others; and (5) what steps must be taken to narrow the divide and resolve the conflict. Ultimately, as a Christian parent or gatekeeper of young people, you probably want to know how best to instill biblical values and morals within your young people in a culture that does not share those values and morals.

We will address each of these areas of division beginning with the two different meanings of tolerance.

UNDERSTANDING TOLERANCE DIFFERENTLY

Remember how Renee in chapter 1 wanted her parents to be tolerant of her sleeping with her boyfriend? The tolerance she was calling for was not a tolerance her parents were willing to give. Chad wants his dad to be tolerant of Mike's brother and the gay community, but Todd doesn't feel right in doing so. This is because, as we mentioned in the previous chapter, there are two distinct concepts of tolerance at play here.

Traditional Tolerance

As we have already noted, cultural tolerance goes far beyond what you might have considered the word to mean.

Webster's defines *tolerate* as "to recognize and respect [other's beliefs, practices, etc.] without sharing them," and "to bear or put up with [someone or something not especially liked]."[5] This attitude is basically what Paul expressed in 1 Corinthians 13:7 when he said that love "endures through every circumstance."

The Bible says, "Live in harmony with each other. . . . Do all that you can to live in peace with everyone" (Romans 12:16, 18). If

Christ *died* for us when we were sinners, surely we can love and serve other sinners like us (Romans 5:6–8). Jesus didn't save us because we were righteous but because of his mercy. Therefore, we have mercy on people, not because they are righteous, but because Jesus had mercy on us. Because of his grace, we now have grace. Christ's grace is the basis of our loving others we disagree with. And when we act this way, we are preaching Christ's grace to the world.

Scripture makes it clear how Christians are to act toward each other and toward those who disagree with them.

> *Always be humble and gentle. Be patient with each other, making allowance for each other's faults because of your love.* (Ephesians 4:2)

> *Be kind to each other, tenderhearted, forgiving one another, just as God through Christ has forgiven you.* (Ephesians 4:32)

> *Make allowance for each other's faults, and forgive anyone who offends you.* (Colossians 3:13)

Traditional tolerance is perfectly compatible with such scriptural commands because the traditional understanding of *tolerance* has meant these things:

- Respecting and protecting the legitimate rights of others, even those with whom you disagree and those who are different from you. Essentially, traditional tolerance means "everyone has a right to his own opinion." Yet when those opinions violate God's moral law to the extent of hurting others, tolerance turns to intolerance. It is this type of intolerance that enabled Christians (and others) to fight for the abolition of slavery in nineteenth-century America, to shelter Jews from Hitler's Nazis, and to be among the leaders in the early civil rights movement in the United States and elsewhere.

- Listening to and learning from other perspectives, cultures, and backgrounds. A Christian teen who respectfully attends a classmate's bar mitzvah is demonstrating traditional tolerance, as is a Westerner who removes her shoes upon entering a Japanese home or a high school student who listens courteously as an exchange student describes his native land, culture, and religion.

- Living peaceably alongside others, in spite of differences. "Work at living in peace with everyone," the Bible says (Hebrews 12:14). The people of God are commanded to be peace seekers (Psalm 34:14), peace promoters (Proverbs 12:20), peacemakers (Matthew 5:9), and peace pursuers (1 Peter 3:11). This does not mean that you must sacrifice godly principles to achieve peace, but it does mean that you are to "do all that you can to live in peace with everyone" (Romans 12:18).

- Building relationships with people regardless of their race, creed, nationality, or sex. After all, Jesus (though a Jew) spoke freely and respectfully to a Samaritan woman (John 4:1–42), shared meals with tax collectors (Matthew 9:9–13), and even touched lepers (Matthew 8:1–4)—all of which were strict taboos for Jewish men of Jesus' day. When a Canaanite woman approached him for a miraculous healing (the Canaanites were historic enemies of the Jewish people and worshipped Baal, Dagon, and other gods), Jesus commended her faith in him and healed her daughter (Matthew 15:21–28). Traditional tolerance exhibits that kind of loving treatment of people as individuals (while not necessarily accepting their beliefs or behavior).

Traditional tolerance values, respects, and accepts the individual *without necessarily* approving of or participating in that person's beliefs or behavior. This is what Renee's parents were attempting to do. While they experienced disappointment in their daughter's decision to sleep with her boyfriend, they still tried to love their daughter. Kenton, her father, especially struggled with finding a proper balance between expressing love and acceptance of his daughter and disapproval of her behavior. While he had no problem making it clear that he couldn't endorse her moral choices, he *did* have a problem making her feel accepted, even though that's how he wanted her to feel. We will discuss in subsequent chapters how we as parents and gatekeepers can achieve and communicate that needed love and acceptance.

Chad's father, Todd, was trying to express his belief that homosexual behavior was wrong and shouldn't be celebrated while at the same time not rejecting gay people. But Chad clearly felt his dad was rejecting the gay community. These parents were attempting to do the right thing by not compromising truth, even though they could have expressed their views in a more gracious and loving manner. In a later chapter we will show how the parents of Chad and Renee end up sincerely expressing love and acceptance without conveying a sense of condemnation.

Cultural Tolerance

Today when you hear the word *tolerance* used, it rarely has the traditional meaning of the word. In our culture tolerance goes beyond acknowledging and respecting the differing beliefs and practices of others. This new tolerance, what we will call *cultural tolerance,* propagates the notion that there is no hierarchy of moral truth—all truth is equal. In traditional tolerance you grant another the right to believe and behave differently without agreeing that he or she is right. Not so with cultural tolerance. What has shifted is the equality of beliefs, values, and truth claims. In other words, not only do all people have a right to believe what they want, but no one's beliefs, values, or truth claims are any more valid than another person's. Essentially, cultural tolerance means all truth is subjective, and thus no individual truth claim should be judged or condemned as wrong.

This understanding of tolerance has been around in our modern culture for some time. Roughly two decades ago Thomas Helmbock was the executive vice president of the national Lambda Chi Alpha fraternity. While not agreeing with this definition, he identified the fraternity's view on tolerance: "Tolerance [today] is that every individual's beliefs, values, lifestyle, and perception of truth claims are equal. . . . There is no hierarchy of truth. Your beliefs and my beliefs are equal, and all truth is relative."[6]

That definition of tolerance, with its belief that moral truth is relative and subjectively determined, has now become institutionalized within culture. From 1995 to 2005 the Barna Group tracked the views of Americans on moral relativism. During that time period, fewer than 32 percent of Christian adults believed in a universal truth, and only 9 percent of professed Christian teens said that universal truth existed.[7] This statistic hasn't changed over the last ten years. "Even among born-again adults," Barna reports, "that statistic has remained flat."[8]

Today most people still believe that the standard for sexual morality is determined by the individual. A 2014 Pew Research Center study found that 29 percent of Americans believe that premarital sex is morally acceptable, with an additional 36 percent saying it's not even a moral issue. This adds up to a total of 65 percent endorsing premarital sex. The same study found that 23 percent believed homosexuality to be acceptable, with another 35 percent saying it's not a moral issue.[9] That's a total of 58 percent of the population endorsing homosexuality as a valid lifestyle. One respondent echoed the feeling of many who read the report. She said, "If you want to poll attitudes toward homosexuality that is one thing, but don't couch it in terms of morality."[10] Why such a response? Because most people have adopted moral relativism and are offended by even the suggestion that morality exists outside ourselves. To the vast majority of our culture, moral truth is subjective and to be decided by the individual.

Renee was the one who decided that sleeping with her boyfriend was right. She believed her decision was personal and should be decided by her and her boyfriend. She felt judged by her parents when they expressed disapproval of her behavior. She felt this way because her parents believed their moral truth on sex before marriage was right and hers was wrong. They accepted the biblical narrative about truth that established a hierarchy of truth and values. What they were "guilty" of was holding up a standard they believed was valid for everyone. This violated the doctrine of cultural tolerance.

Why was Chad upset with his dad? He was angered that Todd stated outright that homosexuality was wrong. That, of course, seemed to him a put-down of Mike's brother. In Chad's eyes, his dad had wrongly set himself up as judge and jury. He felt his father showed disrespect and intolerance of gay people. Todd was trying to stand up for biblical morality, but because his approach was flawed, it inadvertently reinforced to his son the validity of cultural tolerance.

Cultural tolerance says that what every individual believes or says *is* equally right and equally valid, and that no individual's beliefs or behavior should be judged or criticized. That means they believe there is no morality that is right for everyone. With that doctrine, not only do all people have an equal right to their beliefs, but they also have a right to be treated as if their beliefs, as well as the beliefs of all others, are equal. All values are equal. All lifestyles are equal. All truth claims are equal. Violate that tenet of cultural tolerance and you will be labeled judgmental, intolerant, and even a bigot.

Labeling others as intolerant for a differing standard of morality isn't limited to families or colleagues within the business community or the educational system. Throughout Western culture today, a growing number of government legislators are speaking out against ministers, churches, and Christian schools. While technically government isn't allowed to legislate the kind of morality churches and Christian schools adopt, it is beginning to apply pressure that is having the same social effect as legislation.

California legislators in San Francisco wrote a letter to Archbishop Salvatore Cordileone urging him to remove the morality clauses from the Catholic high school teachers' handbook. The morality clause included a stand against sex outside of marriage, pornography, and gay sex. The letter, signed by every San Francisco lawmaker, stated that the church's morality clauses "foment a discriminatory environment" and send "an alarming message of intolerance to youth."[11]

It's not enough for the church to express love and respect toward those who believe and live contrary to biblical morality. To be truly tolerant (culturally tolerant), they and all Christians must agree that another person's opposing position or behavior is right for him—and, in fact, praise him for it. To be caring, accepting, and "tolerant" of Mike's brother and everyone at the Gay Games, Todd needed not only to acknowledge that homosexual behavior was right for them but also to endorse that lifestyle as valid. Todd was free to say being gay wasn't right for himself, but he had no right to say it was wrong for others—that is, according to cultural tolerance.

This is a very difficult place for parents like Todd, Teri, Kenton, and all of us to be. It makes us out to be judgmental, unaccepting, and even arrogant. Who are we to say sleeping with a boyfriend before marriage is wrong? What right have Christians or the church to stand in judgment of gay people, especially if they were born that way? These parents and all of us who hold to a biblical narrative about moral truth, will have an impossible task in countering cultural tolerance as long as our young people look to the culture's narrative about truth to get their standards for morality. The truth is, we are not called to be tolerant of others as the culture defines it; we are called to be loving as the Bible defines it.

The divide between the two definitions of tolerance is centered on these two different narratives of moral truth. Until we move our children to a different premise for determining how they view and understand moral truth, we will almost surely fail to impart a set of biblical values. Understanding the difference between traditional tolerance and cultural tolerance is the first step in reaching our young people with a message of biblical morality. The next step is to understand the nature of moral truth. We need to understand what makes moral truth universal. Why does our culture see it as subjective and relative? How did we get here? How do we get our young people to embrace a biblical morality? When we answer these questions correctly, we will be on the road to some real solutions. That is the task of the chapters that follow.

CHAPTER 3

THE IRONY: INTOLERANCE IN THE NAME OF TOLERANCE

When my daughter, Katie, was in high school, I (Josh) asked her a probing question. I was a little concerned that some students might tease or make fun of her for having a traveling evangelist and youth speaker as a dad.

"Honey," I said, "are you afraid at all of being called any names or labeled in any way at school?"

"Yeah, I am," she responded without hesitation.

"What are you afraid of?"

"I'm afraid of being called intolerant."

The "intolerant" label was enough to strike fear into the heart of my teenage daughter. That was more than twenty years ago, and the cultural environment has only gotten worse since then. Here's the irony: some of the most vocal advocates for tolerance are completely intolerant of those who express their belief in a biblical morality, especially if they do so in the public arena. A case in point: Atlanta mayor Kasim Reed fired Fire Chief Kelvin Cochran for a self-published book Cochran wrote and distributed only to Christians or to those who requested it. In the book, *Who Told You That You Were Naked?*, Cochran defines marriage as a union between a man and a woman and deems homosexuality to be immoral. He cites the Bible as his source for such beliefs.

Cochran's dismissal was based not on his actions toward gays in the workplace but apparently on his personal beliefs. According to one report, "Cochran was, indeed, investigated and exonerated from any charges that he treated gay or lesbian persons on the job disrespectfully at any time during his long career. . . . As Mayor Reed stated, the standard here isn't actual discrimination in the workplace. It is 'fear of being discriminated against,' which he alleges Cochran has spread."[1]

The *New York Times* op-ed page weighed in on the subject with this: "It should not matter that the investigation found no evidence that Mr. Cochran had mistreated gays or lesbians. . . . Nobody can tell Mr. Cochran what he can or cannot believe. If he wants to work as a public official, however, he may not foist his views on other city employees."[2]

Those calling for tolerance of the gay and lesbian lifestyle seem to be intolerant of a fire chief who believes such a lifestyle is immoral, even though there is no evidence he ever discriminated against gay people in the workplace. Mr. Cochran expressed his feelings this way in a speech following his dismissal: "My termination has indeed made a great statement. . . . These statements [that you better keep your mouth shut or you will be fired] are an indictment against our American values and do not embrace the diversity of which we are so proudly boasting of here in our wonderful city of Atlanta. Indeed, a strong statement has been made: all people groups are welcomed and embraced in the city of Atlanta, except the groups that believe the Scripture regarding God's purpose for sex."[3]

Another case involves Barronelle Stutzman, a Washington State floral artist who was successfully sued for refusing to contribute to a same-sex wedding. It wasn't that the florist didn't sell flowers to gay couples—she did. She also employed gay people in her shop. What she was uncomfortable doing was providing her personal creative talents to artistically celebrate a union that her beliefs dictated was not to be celebrated. The state judge ruled that the florist must provide full support for wedding ceremonies that were contrary to her faith.[4]

THE BIBLICAL NARRATIVE ABOUT MORAL TRUTH

Who is being intolerant of whom? There are those who promote diversity and freedom of religion while at the same time exhibiting complete intolerance of those who express their beliefs in an objective, universal moral truth of scripture that establishes guidelines and boundaries for sexual behavior.

To many, stating that the Bible reveals moral truth for everyone sounds narrow and intolerant of people who believe otherwise or live contrary to biblical commands. Few people today like to hear that they are wrong just because they don't align with an ancient book on morality. Renee and Chad chafed under the idea that someone established a set of rules that applies to everyone. They were more comfortable with the idea that each person has the right to create his or her own moral code. That philosophy is a lot less restrictive, and if others can be pressured to endorse it, it will enable all people to do what they want and avoid judgment from others. The thinking is, if people want to choose a biblical morality for themselves, that's their business as long as they keep it quiet. But they should not be allowed to say that those morals are universal.

This type of thinking fails to recognize the origin of morality or understand the true biblical narrative about truth. When we understand what makes moral truth actually moral, it reframes the entire issue of tolerance and intolerance.

The Definition of Truth

The concept of truth often seems abstract or philosophical to the present generation. But when we understand moral truth from the biblical narrative, it becomes innately concrete and relational.

Webster defines truth, in part, as "fidelity to an original or standard; the body of real things, events, or facts; the property of being in accordance with fact or reality."[5]

Let's look at the practical application of that definition of truth. I (Josh) have been known to do a few handyman jobs around the house from time to time. And when I do, I rely on truth and reality. I know, for example, that when I need a six-foot two-by-four, I'll be able to cut the board to the exact length of six feet. How do I know that? I measure the cut board against a standard of measurement—a measuring tape—that conforms to a universal standard that has been established by the International Bureau of Weights and Measures. When the two-by-four board matches correctly the six-foot mark on the measuring tape, which in turn conforms to the original universal standard for six feet, I can truthfully state that it is, in fact, six feet long. Truth conforms precisely to the original or standard.

Truth also is the property of being in accordance with fact or reality. A claim is true if it matches reality. As a kid I (Sean) was always intrigued by luxury, high-end cars like Maseratis and Lamborghinis. I still am. I'll never own one, of course, but their precision, power, and craftsmanship fascinate me. To determine a truth claim about a Maserati, fantasize a moment with me.

Suppose I tell you it is absolutely the truth that my 755 horsepower Maserati MC12 Corsa can go from zero to sixty miles per hour in less than three seconds. You doubt that my statement is true, and you tell me so to my face. I respond, "Hop in, and I'll prove it."

You climb into the passenger seat, and I hand you a stopwatch. I tell you to begin timing me at the moment I accelerate. When I yell, "Sixty," you are to hit the stopwatch. I rev the engine, pop the clutch, and before you know it, I yell, "Sixty!" You look at the stopwatch. It reads 2.9 seconds.

Why is my statement that a Maserati can go from zero to sixty in less than three seconds true? Because it corresponds to reality. The car actually did go from zero to sixty in less than three seconds, so my statement was true. Truth is when our beliefs match up with the objective world. Now how does this relate to knowing what makes moral truth objective and universal? How can we know that certain moral truths apply to everyone? A politician over two thousand years ago posed an interesting question by asking point blank, "What is truth?"

What Is Truth?

After Jesus was arrested, he was brought before Pilate, the Roman governor of Judea. He asked Jesus if he was a king. "Jesus responded, 'You say I am a king. Actually, I was born and came into the world to testify to the truth. All who love the truth recognize that what I say is true'" (John 18:37). It was at that point that Pilate asked, "What is truth?"

The answer to that question would have been clear to Pilate had he been a follower of Jesus. Moral truth isn't simply an abstract concept; it originates in a person who is the original and standard for morality. Jesus said, "I am the way, the truth, and the life" (John 14:6). Moral truth ultimately finds its source in a "who," not merely in a "what." In other words, moral claims are true if they correspond to the character of God—who is the objective source for morality. God is the source of all moral truth. "He is the Rock," Moses said, "his work is perfect. . .a God of truth and without iniquity, just and right is he" (Deuteronomy 32:4 KJV). It is God's nature and character that actually determine moral truth. He defines what is right and wrong, good and evil. But truth is not first and foremost something he decides; it is something he *is*.

The basis of everything we call moral, the Source of every good thing, is the eternal God who is outside us, above us, and beyond us. The apostle James wrote, "Every good and perfect gift is from above, coming down from the Father of the heavenly lights, who does not change like shifting shadows" (James 1:17 NIV).

How would Renee or Chad respond if they knew morality wasn't something they created by their own choice? What if they understood that morality was already in existence in a person who loved and accepted everyone for who he or she is? That would reframe the entire conversation between these young people and their parents. Our young people need to understand that the reason we have this concept that some things are morally right and others are wrong is not because a church propagates it or even that it is written in a book called the Bible. The moral authority of the Bible isn't found in its commands and rules. The authority of scripture is derived directly from and founded in the very character and nature of God and represented in the flesh through Jesus Christ. All moral truth resides in and comes from God.

The reason we think there are such concepts as "fair" and "unfair" is because our Maker is a just God and we have been made in his image (Genesis 1:27).

The reason love is a virtue and hatred a vice is because the God of relationships who formed us is a God of love.

The reason honesty is right and deceit is wrong is because God is true.

The reason fidelity in marriage is honorable and infidelity is not is because God is faithful.

The reason chastity is moral and promiscuity is immoral is because God is pure.

Everything that is moral, right, holy, good, and beautiful comes from the core nature of God. He doesn't choose to do holy and right things as if he is doing an experiment to see what that's like. He does holy and right things because that is who he is—his actions come out of his core nature (Genesis 18:25).

We need to help our young people realize that God's Son, Jesus, is the embodiment of moral truth and that true freedom comes from embracing and living the truth of God (John 8:32). When they come to realize this, they will begin to understand that they cannot create their own brand of morality. Unchangeable morality already exists as a universal truth because it comes from a personal God. We are, however, given the freedom to make a choice—to choose whether we are going to accept Jesus as our universal moral truth and follow in his ways or choose our own way. God has given each of us the freedom to choose truth or falsehood; reality or delusion. We are given the freedom to be wrong—and to suffer the consequences of that choice. Understanding Jesus Christ as the universal and objective embodiment of moral truth means the following:

- Truth cannot be subjectively created; moral truth is and comes from the objective, absolute person of Christ himself. As John wrote, "The law was given through Moses; grace and truth came through Jesus Christ" (John 1:17 NIV).
- Truth cannot be relative and change from person to person or from community to community, because Jesus is the incarnation of the God who "never changes or casts a shifting shadow" (James 1:17). As the scripture says, "Jesus Christ is the same yesterday, today, and forever" (Hebrews 13:8).
- All truth claims cannot be equal because Jesus didn't claim to be "a" truth—one among viable others. His claim was exclusive; he claimed to be the one and only

Truth, the only way to God. "I am the way, the truth, and the life," he said. "No one can come to the Father except through me" (John 14:6, emphasis added). Those are not the words of someone who is "one among many," someone who is "equal" to all others; those are the words of one who has no equal. He is the incarnation of the one who said, "I am the LORD; there is no other God. I have equipped you for battle, though you don't even know me, so all the world from east to west will know there is no other God. I am the LORD, and there is no other" (Isaiah 45:5–6).

The writings of Moses and the Old Testament prophets tell us that morality and moral behavior came from the Lawgiver, God himself. Through these inspired writings, Judaism gave us what we call *ethical theism*—the belief that right and wrong are universal and unchanging, and that a set of moral truths comes from a personal God. We err when we see biblical rules and commands as isolated, separate from God. God gave Moses pages and pages of highly specific rules to govern the relationships and morality of his people. Each of those rules, which we call *precepts*, applies to a specific situation. But each is important because it is grounded in a *principle*, which is a fundamental, primary law from which other laws—the precepts—are derived. Each principle, in turn, is grounded in a *person*—in the very character of God himself.

To illustrate, here is a precept from the book of Exodus: "If someone steals an ox or sheep and then kills or sells it, the thief must pay back five oxen for each ox stolen, and four sheep for each sheep stolen" (22:1). This precept is a specific instance that forbids stealing animals from another person. This precept related to the stealing of animals is grounded in a broader, more inclusive principle of honesty that forbids stealing of any kind, lying, deceit, fraud, and the like. The principle of honesty, however, finds its genesis in the very character of God, who is true and right. "He is a faithful God who does no wrong; how just and upright he is!" (Deuteronomy 32:4). The precepts give us the commands, and the principles give us the "why" behind the commands. But every biblical precept that leads to a broader principle directs us back to the person of God.

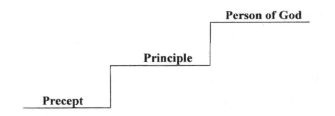

We know that morals are universal when they are grounded in the very nature of God, who is absolutely "righteous in everything he does" (Psalm 145:17), "the one who is holy and true" (Revelation 3:7), and "there is no evil in him" (Psalm 92:15). But God is not behind the principles and precepts simply to validate the rules; he is there as a person for the purpose of relationship.

The Bible says that God spoke to Moses "face to face, as one speaks to a friend" (Exodus 33:11). Afterward Moses prayed, "If you are pleased with me, teach me your ways so I may know you" (Exodus 33:13 NIV). Moses recognized that learning God's ways—understanding his precepts and the principles behind them—would acquaint him with the person of God himself. Ultimately God doesn't simply want our strict obedience to a set of rules and commands. As he told Hosea the prophet, "I want you to show love, not offer sacrifices. I want you to know me more than I want burnt offerings" (Hosea 6:6). This is why Jesus said, "And this is the way to have eternal life—to know you, the only true God, and Jesus Christ, the one you sent to earth" (John 17:3). God wants to be in relationship with his creation.

Obviously we do not live in a culture that sees morality as coming from the Creator God who purposefully created us with intent and design. Yet it was this view of morality that formed the basis for much of Western civilization. We see this explicitly expressed in the US Declaration of Independence: "We hold these truths to be self-evident, that all men are created equal, *that they are endowed by their Creator* with certain unalienable Rights, that among these are Life, Liberty and the pursuit of Happiness" (emphasis added).

Thus we can see that the biblical narrative of moral truth presents God's commands and rules as stepping-stones leading us to know him and what he is like. But the value of moral truth doesn't stop there. It is also a guide for knowing how we are to treat one another. The biblical narrative tells us that humans disobeyed God, which caused them to become a fallen race that is sinful by nature (Jeremiah 17:9; Romans 3:23). God's laws tell us right from wrong and how we are to treat others. As the founding fathers established a new democracy in America, they did so on the premise that humanity was fallen and thus there was a need for a rule of law to curb our natural tendencies to follow our own wants and lusts even to the detriment of others.

Authors Brad Stetson and Joseph Conti, in their book, *The Truth about Tolerance*, make this observation:

The conduct of the American Revolution and the ideology of the American founders show a marked awareness of human fallibility, *that is, a recognition of human fallenness. Russell Kirk [author of* Roots of American Order*] comments on this very distinction: "A principle difference between the American Revolution and the French Revolution was this: the American revolutionaries in general held a biblical view of man and his bent toward sin, while the French revolutionaries in general attempted to substitute for the biblical understanding an optimistic doctrine of human goodness advanced by the philosophers of the rationalistic Enlightenment." Thus the structure of American government takes into account human sinfulness and adopts governmental controls like checks and balances and the separation of powers to rein in the inevitable malevolent expressions of it.[6]*

The founders of our nation were confident about the existence of God and the idea that we fallen humans needed moral guidance derived from him and his Word. They believed that moral rights are universal, even though some governments don't recognize rights as God-given. They didn't believe these moral truths were true merely for them personally or in their time alone; they knew they are enduring truths applicable for all generations—past, present, and future—and that the government exists to protect them.

But something happened—something that had its genesis four hundred years earlier and would eventually undermine ethical theism and eventually bring us to where we are today.

THE CULTURAL NARRATIVE ABOUT MORAL TRUTH

Every systematic thought has to begin from some type of starting point. For centuries in Western culture, that starting point, as we have said, was the character of God as revealed in scripture.

We know that God has also revealed himself in nature (Psalm 19:1–2). So for some thirteen centuries after Christ, the purpose of science and philosophy was to discover God's design. Art, literature, music, and architecture were intended to reflect his glory. Life and death—and the meaning of human existence—were understood in the context of a universe created and governed by God, the fall, and God's grand design to redeem humans and restore all things to what he originally intended. But that all began to change some seven hundred years ago, giving birth to what is known as *modernism*. This view gradually eclipsed ethical theism, beginning during a period of European history now called the *Renaissance*.

The Renaissance began in Italy in the 1300s and, over the course of the next two centuries, spread throughout Europe, lasting through the sixteenth century. The Renaissance was characterized by great strides in literature, learning, art, and architecture. Writers and artists such as Petrarch, Boccaccio, Giotto, and Michelangelo sparked an era of extraordinary human accomplishment. The Renaissance also marked a significant shift in human thought. In contrast to the Middle Ages (in which the major theme of art, literature, and philosophy was glorifying and serving God), Renaissance artists and thinkers began to exalt man and his abilities as the standard of all accomplishment. This shift gave birth to a doctrine called humanism, which stressed human dignity and ability and regarded man as the center of all things, the master of his fate, the captain of his soul—an emphasis that led eventually to an unbiblical view of man and his relationship to his Creator. As this way of thinking began to take hold, men and women's dependence on God as the source of truth and morality began to wane.

The Renaissance may have had minimal impact on human thinking had it not been followed promptly by a period of history known as the *Enlightenment,* or the Age of Reason. The Enlightenment began in the 1600s and lasted through the next century. While the Renaissance mind acknowledged God, many leaders of the Enlightenment (such as Voltaire and Hume) claimed that if there were a God who had created the world, he had no contact with it now—which meant that men and women were left to discover truth on their own; they could expect no help from God. Man had to depend on his powers of reason if he hoped to discern the truth. Standards of right and wrong were not based on the nature and character of God; they were the products of human reasoning. In the Renaissance, man (not God) became central; in the Enlightenment, man's reason became transcendent. The error of the Enlightenment was not in recognizing human reason as a wonderful thing; it was the attempt to crown man's reason as king in God's place.

Two more historical influences have shaped how many modern people—including our own youth—think and act today. The first of these is the *Industrial Revolution.*

The Industrial Revolution overlapped much of the Enlightenment period, extending from the 1700s through the 1800s. It was an explosive period of human productivity and advancement. The inventions, innovations, and improvements of the Industrial Age fueled more than factory furnaces; it stoked the fires of human confidence. The progress that men and women saw all around them encouraged them to look to themselves for hope and guidance. Man no longer felt the need to look upward (to God); he need only look inward (to himself).

The furnaces of the Industrial Revolution still blazed hot when the theories of Charles Darwin, a former theology student, completed the seismic shift that the Renaissance had begun. The publication of Darwin's *The Origin of Species* in 1859 had a profound impact worldwide. His theories presented an alternative to a theistic understanding of origins; God was no longer needed to explain or understand how the world—and humans—came to be. These theories became known as *Darwinism*.

This shift in thinking had succeeded in convincing men and women that they—not God—were the arbiters of truth and morality. Human reason had replaced God as the object of modern man's worship. Human accomplishments had made man arrogant and confident in his own abilities to create good and judge evil. Finally, with the publication and increasing acceptance of Darwin's theories, God became unnecessary and unwelcome—leaving humans free (in their minds, at least) to judge truth, to reach their own conclusions about right and wrong independent of God and his Word. Friedrich Nietzsche took that line of thinking to its logical conclusion and just prior to the dawn of the twentieth century, proclaimed the death of God.

Modernists saw the world through the eyes of science. To a modernist, any truth that could not be observed and experienced—such as spiritual or moral truth—was *subjective* (that is, dependent on the beliefs of the individual subject).

Renee was echoing modernist thought when she told her parents, "There are some things I have to decide for myself. What you guys decided to do before you got married was your choice. I've made my choice, and I wish you guys could respect that and not judge me." But just as ethical theism was supplanted by modernism, modernism has evolved into what some have called *postmodernism*. Postmodernism involves ideas from a variety of different thinkers, and so it is difficult to capture it in a way that is fair to its diversity. Nevertheless, philosopher J. P. Moreland provides a helpful summary of postmodern thought:

> *As a philosophical ideology, postmodernism is primarily a reinterpretation of what knowledge is and what counts as knowledge, though postmodernists don't like to talk in this way. More broadly, it represents a form of cultural relativism about such things as reality, truth, reason, value, linguistic meaning, the self and other notions. On a postmodern view, there is no such thing as objective reality, truth, value, reason, and so forth. All these are social constructions, creations of linguistic practices, and as such are relative not to individuals, but to social groups that share a narrative.*[7]

While there undoubtedly are some postmodern elements throughout our society and young people are influenced by them to varying degrees, philosopher William Lane Craig points out that we don't actually live in a postmodern culture because "it would be utterly unlivable. People are not relativistic when it comes to matters of science, engineering, and technology; rather, they are relativistic and pluralistic in matters of *religion* and *ethics*. But, of course, that's not postmodernism; that's modernism!"[8]

Even though postmodern thought is prevalent in certain circles today, such as in the belief that gender is fluid, it seems that our culture may best be described as *hypermodern*. Modern thought has not disappeared and in fact still reigns. There is more confidence in human reason, and especially science, than ever before. With the explosion of information, technology, and transportation, there seems to be a newfound confidence that new horizons will arise through the growth of science. For instance, the March 2015 cover story for *National Geographic* was about the so-called war on science. The author argues that while there are certain people who don't want to accept the findings of science—such as those who reject climate change, evolution, and the moon landing—science is the one discipline that can really provide truth about the world.[9] According to this article, there seems to be a newfound belief that science is the one sure discipline that can actually explain the world we live in and help transform it for good (even if some stubborn "science deniers" won't join the bandwagon). This confidence in science also appears in films such as *Interstellar* (Warner Brothers Pictures and Paramount Pictures, 2014). The twist (warning: spoiler) is that the role of the savior unexpectedly ends up being taken not by an alien or a supernatural being, but by human beings and science. We are our own hope and shouldn't look to anything else to save us. The confidence in science is on clear display, as it is in many other popular cultural mediums such as books, magazines, television, and of course, online.

While the massive amount of information available through the Internet today undoubtedly fosters skepticism, there is an enduring belief that science can deliver truth. History and math are also seen as disciplines that can deliver truth. And yet when it comes to religion and morality, relativism reigns. As William Lane Craig observed, this is not postmodernism, but modernism. We don't hear young people saying, "Who are you to judge?" or "That's just your truth," when talking about science. But they do say that about morality. Why? Because while they believe scientific claims must conform to the standard of reality, they don't understand there is a standard of moral reality they must conform to as well.

Your children may be influenced to varying degrees by modernism and postmodernism, but it doesn't mean they will soon be rejecting God. Believing in God, even the God of the Bible, is not a problem for most young people today. It's just that they feel free to define him and his truth on their own terms—which means they will shape truth to fit their own personal desires. They act as if God gives them the right to see him through the lens of their own cultural and life experiences. They can mix and match the kind of God, morals, and religion that best allows them to do what they want to do.

How does that kind of view cause a person to interpret the Bible? What kind of values, convictions, and faith does that tend to generate in our hypermodernist culture? How are our young people being shaped by the culture around them, and what can you do about it? Read on for some surprising answers.

CHAPTER 4

WHEN ANYTHING GOES

How do young people today define sexual morality? Do they believe two unmarried teenagers are actually having sex when they engage in oral sex? Does reaching the age of eighteen make having premarital intercourse okay? Who defines virginity? Who determines whether sexual activity is right or wrong? Is porn really such a big deal? Where do most of our young people find their moral compass?

For sixteen-year-old Samantha, sexual intercourse is okay at age eighteen. "My boyfriend and I talked sex over," she said, "and we both agreed that doing it [sexual intercourse] sometime in our senior year (two years from now) would be a good decision."[1] According to Samantha, premarital sexual intercourse is right for her at the "appropriate" age.

Samantha is a typical sixteen-year-old who wrote anonymously about what she thinks defines sex and virginity. She and her boyfriend engage in oral sex but do not define that as "having sex." She says, "People have begun saying that oral sex is a type of sex, so I have had sex and that I am no longer a virgin, but I find this very inaccurate. I think people should have their own view on what their virginity is." Samantha goes on to explain that to her, virginity is "a frame of mind." She concludes, "Right now I consider myself half a virgin. . . . Until you have felt the full thrill and intimacy of sex to its greatest extent with someone you truly love, you are still a virgin in my mind, but maybe that's just me."[2]

This sixteen-year-old determines for herself the definition of virginity and when it's right to engage in sex. Her moral compass is aligned with a cultural narrative about truth. Her attitude represents that of the majority of young people today. In the minds of most teenagers, there is no universal standard for sexual morality or absolutes beyond a person's own view as to what makes sexual activity right or wrong. As Samantha said, "I think people should have their own view," and, "and we both agreed that doing it sometime in our senior year would be a good decision."

This perspective is reflected in such oft-heard statements as these:

- "No one has the right to tell me what's right or wrong for me."
- "I can't tell you what's right or wrong; you must decide that for yourself."
- "It's wrong to try to impose your morals on someone else."
- "I have the right to do whatever I want as long as I'm not hurting anyone."
- "Those may be the values your parents taught you, but my parents taught me different."
- "Look. . .that's *your* opinion."
- "Listen to your heart."

When moral truth becomes a matter of opinion, personal preference, or the individual's views and feelings, then practically anything goes. Recently an article surfaced in a mainstream magazine about a forty-two-year-old man's obsession with having sex with a horse. He insisted, "There's nothing wrong with it." After he shared his sexual preference with a clinical psychologist, she concurred with him and stated that he didn't need treatment for his "attraction."[3] In a culture of tolerance where the individual decides morality, morality has no bounds.

Cultural tolerance has had a significant influence on this generation in a number of areas but most notably in the area of sex.

Mary Eberstadt, an author and senior fellow at the Ethics and Public Policy Center, makes this point: "Rather than a product of any rich philosophical tradition, the new tolerance is, at root, about sex; it's a descendent of the sexual revolution."[4] That is certainly the case, and we will deal in more depth with the sexual aspect of morality in later chapters. Yet the damaging influence of cultural tolerance is not limited to sexual morality. We need to be aware of how an "anything goes" culture is influencing our children's perception of the authority of the Bible, their concept of what is virtuous, their ideas of honor and courage, and even their understanding of justice. All of these values, for the most part, have been shaped by the culture rather than scripture. The Bible is the very foundation on which our faith and morals rest. When that foundation is eroded, almost anything goes.

HOW AUTHORITATIVE IS THE BIBLE?

As we have said, cultural tolerance propagates the view that all religious beliefs and moral truth claims are equal and individually determined. While many young people from Christian homes accept that viewpoint, they will at the same time assert that the Bible provides a description of moral truth. That may at first seem contradictory because it doesn't make sense to believe we create our own subjective moral truth while at the same time believing the Bible to be the source of objective moral truth.

The explanation of this apparent contradiction centers on whether you use a definite or indefinite article. To you perhaps the Bible is *the* source of moral truth, even though you likely value tradition, the wisdom of elders, the conclusion of experts, and a variety of other sources. To many of our young people it is *a* source of moral truth. In other words, the Bible is not considered to be authoritatively true for everyone. It is only true and authoritative to those who choose to believe it to be so. Therefore, if each of us is responsible for creating his or her own truth, then it follows that the Bible may be one's chosen reference guide in developing one's own brand of morality. This is how many Christian young people see the Bible today.

The doctrine of cultural tolerance has taught our young people to view the Bible quite differently from the way you probably view scripture. They see the Bible *not* as a universally true revelation of the one true God but as a mere resource, a set of inspirational stories and helpful insights that offer guidance in creating one's own "truth." That helps to explain why many Christian young people adhere to some biblical standards but violate others. We've talked to thousands of young people who say that adultery is wrong but premarital sex is okay. As a youth speaker and part-time high school teacher, I (Sean) have seen many young people who claim to be pro-life take a friend to an abortion clinic when she's in trouble. Many of them honestly think they are doing the right thing even though their choices violate the teachings of scripture. This is no doubt how Samantha views the Bible. She and an entire generation tend to go to the Bible *not to discover the truth* and bend their lives to it accordingly but to use it as sort of a self-help book to help them form their own version of what's true and false, good and evil, right and wrong. And sadly, this is a growing trend among older generations of Christians, too.

On a recent episode of *Super Soul Sunday* with Oprah Winfrey, former mega-church pastor Rob Bell claimed that the Christian church will become irrelevant if it doesn't quickly reject some of its antiquated teachings. When asked by Oprah if the church is "moments away" from embracing same-sex marriage, Bell replied,

"Absolutely. . .I think culture is already there, and the church will continue to be even more irrelevant when it quotes letters from 2,000 years ago as their best defense."[5] In other words, the Bible is an antiquated book that the church must ignore or face irrelevance.

Most people in today's culture see the Bible primarily as a religious book that arose from the religions of Judaism and Christianity. In their minds, these are merely two among many viable religions in the world. The Hebrew Bible (the Old Testament) is considered to contain the religious views of the Jewish people. The New Testament lays out the religious views of Christianity and its founder, Jesus. If you choose to adhere to Judaism or Christianity, you are free to glean from their religious teachings and rituals as you like. Or you can choose from hundreds of other world religions and their subdivided groups. In fact, you can pick and choose your beliefs smorgasbord style and create a religion tailor-made just for you. It doesn't really matter what religion or religious book you choose to believe; the one universal truth is that you have the right to create your own truth.

If this thinking has influenced your children, and it probably has, how do you counter it? Can you just come right out and say, "Wait just a minute! What the Bible teaches constitutes the only true religion in the world. If you don't believe the Bible, I'm sorry, but your beliefs are just dead wrong." As you can imagine, taking that approach is not a wise choice. The responses of the fathers of Renee and Chad in our earlier stories demonstrate that a reactive, us-versus-them approach is rarely successful. Having been influenced to believe it's up to the individual to *create* his or her own truth, our young people are naturally uncomfortable with any suggestion that one particular viewpoint is true for everyone. That discomfort is understandable in the light of how they think of the Bible—as an optional set of religious teachings adopted by a particular religious group. Of course this is not what the Bible is or what it's about. But since our young people are operating from a different viewpoint, it is important that we take that viewpoint into consideration when we talk to them about truth, morality, and biblical authority.

When you discuss the Bible, do not refer to it simply as a spiritual book that teaches us how to live, but as a road map leading one toward the discovery of true reality. The biblical narrative about moral truth teaches that the Creator God revealed himself to Moses and the prophets at given points in history. While the Bible contains poetry, psalms, apocalyptic literature, and parables, it is ultimately a true account of God's relationship with humanity. Moses and the other writers of scripture documented their encounters and messages from God, and these encounters are substantiated by historical evidences and fulfilled prophecy.

Yes, scripture is the source of Judaism and Christianity, which are religions. Yet the Bible is unique among all other religious writings in that it is based on historical events backed up by credible historical evidence. The Creator of the world revealed himself first to Moses and the prophets saying, "I am the LORD; there is no other God. I have equipped you. . .so all the world from east to west will know there is no other God. I am the LORD, and there is no other" (Isaiah 45:5–6). He then took on flesh and revealed himself in the person of Jesus, God's Son. The New Testament writer said, "Long ago God spoke many times and in many ways to our ancestors through the prophets. And now in these final days, he has spoken to us through his Son. God promised everything to the Son as an inheritance, and through the Son he created the universe" (Hebrews 1:1–2).

The one true God's communication to humanity and the whole of Christianity as a religion is based on three primary realities supported by evidences. These are often referred to as the pillars of the faith. These pillars, as listed below, need to be taught and ingrained within our young people.

- *The historic reliability of scripture.* "All Scripture is inspired by God" (2 Timothy 3:16). Scripture is not merely an inspirational book. All scripture is "God-breathed," which means the written words in the Bible are from Creator God. Since its words come from God, the Bible can be trusted as a reliable historical document, and we have credible evidence to substantiate that reality.
- *The deity of Christ.* We also have credible historical evidence to back up Christ's claim that he was and is the Son of God "who takes away the sin of the world" (John 1:29). If Christ is not who he claims to be, Christianity is not true.
- *Christ's bodily resurrection.* Without Christ literally rising from the dead, his promise to give those who trust in him eternal life would be meaningless. The apostle Paul put it this way, "If Christ has not been raised, then your faith is useless and you are still guilty of your sins. In that case, all who have died believing in Christ are lost" (1 Corinthians 15:17–18). But Christ did rise from the dead, and compelling historical evidence supports this reality.

If the Bible can be proven to be historically inaccurate, if Christ's claim to be God is not historically credible, and if Christ's resurrection can be shown to be a hoax, then Christianity is not a religion worth trusting in. By this view there are certainly good moral teachings in the Bible on how to live and treat one another. But without assurance of the authenticity of Christ's deity, death, and resurrection, they are nothing more. If the Bible were no more than that, it could offer no hope of a life after death. The apostle Paul concluded that if Christ wasn't who he claimed to be and did not bodily rise from the dead "we are more to be pitied than anyone in the world" (1 Corinthians 15:19).

But of course that is not the case. Considerable evidence exists to prove that the God-breathed words of scripture are historically reliable. And when you share those evidences with your children, they inevitably come face-to-face with the claims of Christ. At that point, if they're honest with themselves, they will encounter an inescapable conclusion: *scripture accurately reveals that Jesus is the risen Christ and the only way to the one true God.* Of course, that conclusion flies in the face of their cultural conditioning. But with repeated emphasis on how the Bible is historically accurate and reliable, you will likely be able to equip your children to see God's Word for what it is—a true revelation of the one true God and his Son Jesus as the Savior of the world.

As a university student and skeptic, I (Josh) didn't just have doubts about the validity of Christianity; I set out to disprove it. Specifically, I wanted to show that the Bible is historically unreliable and that Jesus was by no means the resurrected Son of God. I knew that Christ, with his claims to be God, was the linchpin of Christianity. So I reasoned that if the historical document containing the evidence of Christ's virgin birth, his miracles, his messianic prophecies, and his resurrection could be exposed as inaccurate, then the foundation of Christianity would surely crumble. If I could show that the Bible is historically unreliable, I could invalidate all the claims of Christ, including his purported resurrection.

I failed in that quest, of course, because the evidences I discovered convinced me that the Bible is historically reliable— unquestionably so. And that is when I came face-to-face with the awesome truth that God's Word is his revelation to the human race. He wanted to communicate his merciful and masterful plan to the world to redeem his lost children and restore them to a relationship with him for all eternity. I saw that his message was for me. Eventually I placed my trust in Christ, and he transformed me into his redeemed child. Since that time I have been sharing his message and the truth that God's Word is reliable, Christ's claims are verifiably true, and Christ's resurrection is backed up by credible evidence. In fact, I authored a book specifically to help deepen your conviction in the reliability of scripture. It is entitled *God-Breathed* (Barbour Publishing, 2015). Its purpose is to help you bring your children face-to-face with the undeniable power and historical reliability of God's Word.

Let your young people know the Bible isn't a mere resource or a set of inspirational stories and helpful guidelines from which we can form "our own truth." It is the means by which the one true God has chosen to reveal details of himself to each of us. When we hold a Bible in our hands, we are cradling a holy book to be reverenced and hungered after because its reliable words reveal the God who offers us eternal life. Showing that the Bible is the true, inspired Word of God is an important first step. But the ultimate question is whether we will personally obey God's teaching. Do we *really* consider the Bible an authoritative moral source for how we live our lives? Will we follow God's truth even if it makes us uncomfortable, unpopular, and upset?

HOW VIRTUOUS ARE VIRTUES?

Another thing cultural tolerance influences is our concept of virtues. There are certain ideals, such as honor, integrity, courage, respect, self-control, and civility, that we all admire and want our young people to embrace and emulate. We have an innate sense of what these virtues are and how they are reflected in a person's life.

We, and our culture at large, know that it is honorable to defend our nation against terrorist regimes and dictators who threaten our freedom. As a nation that upholds the rule of law, we are to honor and promote the good, defend the rights of freedom of speech and freedom of religion, and seek to protect the citizenry against lawlessness and corruption.

Those who advocate cultural tolerance no doubt agree with that position. They too are interested in the advancement of these virtues around the world. What many may not realize, however, is how the doctrine of cultural tolerance undermines the very virtues they claim to uphold.

While we all may have a sense of what is evil and what is good, under the philosophy of cultural tolerance, evil and good can only be *relative* ideals. Without an objective truth—a set of universal moral values—good and evil are defined by the individual, community, or society. Therefore we have no moral basis by which to judge another person, community, or nation for what they do or don't do.

We as a society are, for the most part, appalled at the atrocities of terrorist groups like ISIS (Islamic State of Iraq and Syria), Al Qaeda, Hamas, and dozens of others that kill innocent men, women, and children in the name of their cause. Yet without a belief in and adherence to an objective and universal moral truth, who is to say that what they do is wrong? Don't they have the same right to choose their own morality as Chad and Renee? Aren't Chad and

Renee forced by their philosophy of cultural tolerance to endorse and celebrate the choices of these terrorist groups and their right to make them?

This is the very dilemma Europe currently faces with the growing Islamization of their continent. British prime minister David Cameron has proclaimed the death of multiculturalism and has called Muslims to embrace British values, such as freedom and equality. "Under the doctrine of state multiculturalism, we have encouraged different cultures to live separate lives, apart from each other and the mainstream," Mr. Cameron said. "We have failed to provide a vision of society to which they feel they want to belong."[6] And yet the deeper question is where Britain got these values *in the first place*.

Social ethics professors Brad Stetson and Joseph Conti get to the heart of the issue: "It is the Judeo-Christian moral tradition of western culture—with its moral realism and commitment to transcultural and transpersonal truth—that decisively has the conceptual resources to mandate [traditional] tolerance and consistently denounce immoral practices."[7] Even the notorious atheist philosopher Friedrich Nietzsche recognized human equality "as another Christian concept" that "furnishes the prototype of all theories of equal rights."[8] More recently, Luc Ferry, also an atheist philosopher, stated bluntly that the Christian notion of equality was "unprecedented at the time, and one to which our world owes its entire democratic inheritance."[9] Even though Christians have been imperfect in their practice of tolerance, Christianity *itself* provides the only suitable basis for tolerance and human rights.

Take advantage of current events to talk to your children about what makes terrorist acts wrong. We are asked to be tolerant of what everyone else believes, so why aren't we tolerant of terrorists? In fact, make the point that intolerance of terrorism is appropriate. We *ought* to *in*tolerate terrorism because terrorism wantonly destroys. God is the author of life. The Destroyer is one of Satan's names. This line of reasoning should help you lead your young people to the inescapable conclusion that unless there are objective and universal moral values, like those that reside in the character of God, no one really has the right to judge even the worst atrocities of terrorists. It is only because the eternal God is righteous by his nature and has revealed himself to us in his Word that we have the basis for knowing that evil (that which does harm) is categorically evil and that honorable men and women are categorically honorable.

Former Minnesota governor Jesse Ventura was highly criticized when he spoke out against the late Chris Kyle. Kyle wrote the bestselling autobiography *American Sniper*. The book sold millions and was adapted into an Oscar-nominated movie. Kyle was a decorated US Navy SEAL and the most lethal sniper in US military history. He served four tours in the Iraq War and was credited with 160 confirmed kills. He was considered an honorable serviceman and a hero by most—but not by Jesse Ventura.

On a radio call-in show, Ventura made this statement in reference to sniper Chris Kyle: "A hero is not how many people you've killed. . . . Do you think the Nazis had heroes? . . . When they invaded France, and if a Nazi soldier killed a hundred people that had lived there, would he be classified a hero in Germany?"[10] Ventura's questioning seems harsh and disrespectful of US servicemen. But to be consistent, those who accept cultural tolerance would have to agree that a Nazi sniper, an Al Qaeda terrorist, or a Hamas bomber would be considered honorable heroes by their respective governments and organizations as well. A Nazi sniper is being courageous for fighting for his fatherland.

An ISIS or Al Qaeda terrorist is convinced that he is advancing a just and holy war against evil infidels in the world. Most modern-day terrorists claim God is on their side and their murderous acts are just.

The point is, under cultural tolerance we cannot say for certain who is truly honorable and just. It all depends on what values one chooses to believe in, and that choice is solely up to the individual—there is no objective morality. And this is true for societies as well as individuals. If culture were the basis of morality, then we could never morally condemn cultures that mistreat women, abuse gays, or kill infidels.

When we ground our morality in the God of the Bible, however, we can clearly judge terrorism as evil. Certainly many atheists also believe terrorism is wrong and are quick to condemn it. The question is not whether they *believe* it is wrong, but what *source* they rely on to make that judgment. Our friend Frank Turek observes, "To have an unchanging objective standard of justice, you don't need molecules—you need an objective, unchanging judge who has supreme authority. Humans can't provide that. Human beings are changeable and do not hold absolute authority over other human beings. You need God for that. If there is no God above Hitler and every other human being, who says murder is wrong?"[11] Turek makes the point that since atheists have no objective standard for morality, they must borrow from the Judeo-Christian worldview when they make moral judgments. For more on this topic, see Frank Turek, *Stealing from God* (Carol Stream, IL: Navpress, 2014).

When we lead our young people to the conclusion that moral values come from a God who is perfectly just and righteous, they can know which virtues are truly virtuous. Because God has given us a clear standard for human attitudes and actions in his Word, we can discover what is truly honorable, courageous, and right.

HOW JUST IS JUSTICE?

If moral truth is subjective and relative, then concepts such as justice are dangerous. If there is no moral code above human beings by which to ground objective human value and responsibility, a virtue like justice for all is subject to the whims of a voting majority or a powerful minority.

Let's say I (Sean) sell you my imaginary Maserati for the ridiculously low, low price of $5,000 cash. You are elated with your bargain until police show up at your door to confiscate the car. They tell you it is actually a stolen vehicle. You claim innocence because you thought you had purchased a car with a clear title. You take me to court to exact justice, only to find out I "own city hall." The courts, the police, and the politicians are in alliance with my corrupt scam to steal cars, sell them for a low price, and have them confiscated by a corrupt police force. You would quickly conclude that justice could not be rendered for everyone as long as a powerful majority is corrupt.

Unless justice is rooted in a moral authority beyond those with the most power or even with the most votes, there cannot be true justice for all. History provides countless examples of injustice when a powerful minority decided to take undue advantage of the weak or the majority in a society failed to protect the rights of the minority. Unless a majority group or a powerful minority commit to a higher moral code beyond themselves, justice will fail. Human slavery is a graphic illustration of how justice miserably fails to protect a minority in absence of adherence to a higher moral code.

The Babylonian Code of Hammurabi records that as far back as the eighteenth century BC the human slave trade was an established institution. From then until the mid-1800s, slavery was a common practice in most countries, including America. Was justice being served even though a majority of the world's communities condoned it? No! Even though people believed slavery was okay, the dignity of African-Americans and all others who were enslaved was being violated nonetheless. In America our collective sense of morality now condemns the enslavement of another person. Yet for centuries "civilized" communities permitted it, and even now human trafficking and bond slavery still exist in many parts of the world. Only a higher, more righteous source of morality can ground true justice, and that source is the holy and just God of the Bible. "Righteousness and justice are the foundation of your throne. Unfailing love and truth walk before you as attendants" (Psalm 89:14).

It's from God, not ourselves, that we find true justice. Yet in the view of some, the God of the Old Testament and Christianity in general is not concerned at all about justice in the world. They see Christianity as an evil empire imposing its will on the masses and threatening to suppress the free expressions of humanity. The late Christopher Hitchens, an outspoken atheist, said, "Religion poisons everything."[12] Famed nineteenth-century atheist Friedrich Nietzsche claimed that Christianity "seeks to work the ultimate corruption, nothing untouched by its depravity; it has turned every value into worthlessness, and every truth into a lie, and every integrity into baseness of the soul."[13] These strong accusations could not be further from the truth.

Although there are those past and present who, under the banner of Christianity, have waged war against the innocent, enslaved people, and otherwise brought disgrace on the name of

Christ, this is only a small, sad corner of the whole picture. And fair-minded people understand that those who committed these evils violated the clear teachings of Jesus. Though these "Christians" were guilty, Christianity itself was innocent, condemning their practices as clearly wrong.

From God's interaction with Adam and Eve, Noah, Abraham, Moses, and the early church, it was understood and taught that life was sacred at every stage. Justice, charity, and human rights are grounded in the fact that we are created in God's image with value, dignity, and worth.

The beauty of God's intolerance of injustice was evident when he spoke through his prophet Amos with this message: "This is what the LORD says: 'The people of Israel have sinned again and again, and I will not let them go unpunished! They sell honorable people for silver and poor people for a pair of sandals. They trample helpless people in the dust and shove the oppressed out of the way'" (Amos 2:6–7).

God put the concept of slavery, more accurately *servitude*, into perspective for his nation Israel. Because God was intolerant of human abuse, he provided guidelines for how foreigners would be treated: "Do not take advantage of foreigners who live among you in your land. Treat them like native-born Israelites, and love them as you love yourself. Remember that you were once foreigners [slaves] living in the land of Egypt. I am the LORD your God" (Leviticus 19:33–34).

Since slaves were often foreigners, they were to be treated like employees by Israel rather than as property to be mistreated. "You must not mistreat or oppress foreigners in any way. Remember, you yourselves were once foreigners in the land of Egypt" (Exodus 22:21). God's constant reminder of what it felt like to be oppressed in Egyptian slavery was a reminder of the need to treat everyone with human dignity.

Slaves in Israel had a high degree of status, rights, and protection unheard of in the ancient Near East. Scholars universally recognize this fact. Slaves were included in religious life, were granted a weekly Sabbath rest (that is, had a day off), had to be set free if bodily harm was inflicted on them, and had the opportunity for freedom every seven years.[14] Furthermore, God condemns slave traders in the New Testament (1 Timothy 1:9–11).

It can be demonstrated that God's mercy and justice as our model has fostered societal justice and provided more positive contributions to society in general than any other force in history.

Atheists and other detractors of Christianity often fail to point out that it is the natural propensity of humans to be self-centered and think only of themselves that has brought such misery and suffering on the masses. The core problem is our broken human nature. The gospel is actually the antidote to this propensity, for it is only through transformation by the Spirit that our natures can be made new (2 Corinthians 5:17).

Greed, corruption, abuse of power, and a basic disregard for others spring from self-centeredness. As Jesus said and history demonstrates, evil comes from within the human heart (Mark 7:14–23). Left unchecked, human nature will always revert to self-serving ways that seek to gain at another's expense. On the opposite side of the moral spectrum, making the interest and care of others as important as your own creates goodwill and harmony and meets human need. This is at the center of Jesus' moral teaching—it represents the very heart of God's nature. Jesus said, "Do to others whatever you would like them to do to you. This is the essence of all that is taught in the law and the prophets" (Matthew 7:12).

Looking out for the interests of others—especially those in need—is the core value of Jesus' message and the basis for true justice. We are to humble ourselves to be servants to others *because* Jesus humbled himself to the point of death for us. According to the apostle Paul, "Let each of you look not only to his own interests, but also to the interests of others. Have this mind among yourselves, which is yours in Christ Jesus, who, though he was in the form of God, did not count equality with God a thing to be grasped, but emptied himself, by taking the form of a servant, being born in the likeness of men. And being found in human form, he humbled himself by becoming obedient to the point of death, even death on a cross" (Philippians 2:4–8 ESV). The sacrifice of Jesus is at the center of Christianity and is the basis for our putting the interests of others above ourselves.

This sense of justice fostered by adherence to the commands of the God of justice is a radical message now, and it was certainly so during the time of Christ. Within the Roman Empire during the first century, enslaving others was commonplace. Abortion was rampant. Parents abandoned virtually all babies that were deformed or otherwise unwanted. Women had few rights.

Yet during this time James, a disciple of Jesus, made a radical statement: "Pure and genuine religion in the sight of God the Father means caring for orphans and widows in their distress and refusing to let the world corrupt you" (James 1:27). These early Christians rejected the cultural practice of allowing abandoned babies and orphaned children to die on the streets. Instead, they would pick them up and adopt them into their own homes. What caused them to do this? It was a morality derived from a higher moral code than their own preferences—it was from God. The intolerance of the early Christians was a beautiful thing. They believed that everyone—including the poor, the homeless, the handicapped, the sick—was made in the image of God with dignity and worth. They were utterly intolerant of injustice, and they did whatever they could to correct the injustices they saw in society.

If we were to highlight just a few of the positive influences that biblical morality has had on justice and caring for others, they would include the following:

- the high value of human life
- care for the sick in creating hospitals
- literacy and education for the masses
- abolition of slavery in the Western world
- the elevation of women
- high standards of justice and civil liberties
- benevolence and charity work

Cultural tolerance, with its claims of equality and justice, falls woefully short of promoting true justice. Real justice is found in God and our adherence to his Word. When talking with your young people, use examples such as slavery, human trafficking, racism, and other forms of human oppression to help your young people understand this vital point. The idea that all concepts of truth are equal and determined by the individual cannot lead to a system of justice for all. That can only be accomplished by an adherence to the Author of true justice. The psalmist put it best when he wrote: "He gives justice to the oppressed and food to the hungry. The LORD frees the prisoners. The LORD opens the eyes of the blind. The LORD lifts up those who are weighed down. The LORD loves the godly. The LORD protects the foreigners among us. He cares for the orphans and widows, but he frustrates the plans of the wicked"

(Psalm 146:7–9).

The doctrine of cultural tolerance undermines the authority of scripture, provides no foundation for what is truly virtuous, and offers no real basis for justice. But perhaps the greatest damage cultural tolerance is inflicting on the thinking of this generation is in the area of sexual morality—especially as it relates to the meaning of love, acceptance, and sexual boundaries. The previous stories of Renee and her parents and Chad and his father offer us an ongoing illustration in the chapters to follow on how to counter cultural tolerance's distortions of love and sex.

CHAPTER 5

LOVE MAKES
IT RIGHT

"What are we gonna do?" Teri asked Kenton soon after their daughter, Renee, was out of the room.

"What do you mean what are *we* gonna do?" Kenton responded. "The question is, what is our daughter going to do? Is she going to continue to go against what we have taught her and live an immoral life, or is she going to wake up and do what's right?"

"No, Kenton," Teri countered, "I'm not talking about Renee; I'm talking about us. If we hold the line too hard, we may push our own daughter right out of our lives."

"That's ridiculous," Kenton retorted. "The issue here is Renee's choices, not ours. We're not pushing her out of our lives; she is the one moving away from our moral values. If she doesn't want to honor our values and God's Word on sexual morality, that's her choice!"

"I guess you're right," Teri replied as she wiped a tear from her eye. "But I think we need to be more understanding and maybe not push our standards so hard on her. You know, she says she loves Tony."

"I thought we were together on this." There was a note of surprise in Kenton's voice.

"We are together, Kenton. I'm just saying we've got to show more love and understanding toward her. If the two of them are really in love, who are we to say they shouldn't at some point be together?"

"Are you saying it's okay for them to sleep together because they think they're in love?"

"Well, if they're really in love and get married eventually, then yeah, I guess so."

"Come on, Teri, let's be together on this and take a stand," Kenton pleaded.

"I'm taking a stand for our daughter," Teri responded. "The important thing is to let Renee know that we love her." With that Teri headed upstairs to console her daughter.

WHAT KIND OF LOVE IS NEEDED?

Teri and Kenton are not unlike a lot of parents whose children no longer share their values regarding sexual morality. For Renee, sleeping with her boyfriend is okay because they love each other. For Kenton, premarital sex is wrong because the Bible teaches it is wrong, period. While Teri agrees with Kenton to a point, she is concerned that the harshness of a rigid position will alienate her daughter from them.

This couple is reacting at opposite sides of the issues of truth and tolerance. Kenton wants to uphold the truth about sexual morality. What he tends to see is primarily the wrongness of his daughter's behavior. Teri, on the other hand, is focusing more on the relationship. She feels the need to be understanding and more tolerant of her daughter's position, even if that means backing off of not permitting Renee to sleep with her boyfriend while he is staying in their home. Maintaining her relationship with Renee is paramount, and she is willing to compromise a bit to keep from severing it.

On the surface, Teri's response appears to be the more loving approach. She too has been influenced by a cultural tolerance that is portrayed as the most loving way to treat someone. It is largely associated in people's minds with such things as kindness, peace, cooperation, understanding, acceptance, even love. To validate someone else's behavior or beliefs is depicted as the loving thing to do.

In light of the message of cultural tolerance, Kenton's position feels harsh and relationally cold. He fears that showing too much acceptance would compromise the truth he holds about what is morally right. Consequently, he does become relationally cold. But rules of morality (truth) were never meant to be expressed coldly— that is, outside the context of a loving and understanding relationship with another who differs with you (traditional tolerance). Rules and relationships, truth and traditional tolerance, love and boundaries were meant to be expressed in perfect harmony with each other.

Cultural tolerance, however, has distorted the idea of relationships and love. It advocates the equality of all moral truth and asserts that no one has the right to hold up a standard of morality for all. And in the process, cultural tolerance twists and distorts the true essence of what love is.

Real love isn't an unlimited endorsement of just any behavior a person chooses to engage in. Many of those behaviors are inherently and inevitably harmful, and to endorse, approve, and encourage them is not loving; it is cold and uncaring. If we care about another person, we won't approve behavior that is damaging and destructive to that person's life. On the other hand, expressing real love doesn't mean condemning people when we find their behavior objectionable and contrary to scripture. Real love— biblical, Godlike love—exposes cultural tolerance as the counterfeit of love because cultural tolerance fails to point people to a universal standard of morality designed to save them from serious harm. Cultural tolerance does not address what is in the best interest of a person—it possesses no moral standard that aligns to what is universally right and good. Real love, on the other hand, looks out for the best interest of others, and sometimes that kind of love will mean addressing destructive choices and behaviors in the people we love. As A. W. Tozer observed, "When we become so tolerant that we lead people into mental fog and spiritual darkness, we are not acting like Christians—we are acting like cowards."[1]

TRUTH AS A BEST FRIEND

God gives us clear moral commands and boundaries in his Word. While they may at first appear restrictive and negative, they are actually freeing and positive. God didn't concoct a set of rules just to be a killjoy or to throw his weight around; he gave rules because he cares about us and wants us to be content and live fulfilled lives that bring glory and honor to him (John 10:10). He knew, for example, that sexual immorality is a path, not to lasting fulfillment, but to emptiness and frustration.

King David and his own son King Solomon understood the value of God's commands when they wrote the following passages:

Joyful are people of integrity, who follow the instructions of the Lord. Joyful are those who obey his laws and search for him with all their hearts. (Psalm 119:1–2)

Make me walk along the path of your commands, for that is where my happiness is found. (Psalm 119:35)

This is how I spend my life: obeying your commandments. (Psalm 119:56)

My child, listen to what I say, and treasure my commands. Tune your ears to wisdom, and concentrate on understanding. . . . Then you will understand what is right, just, and fair, and you will find the right way to go. For wisdom will enter your heart, and knowledge will fill you with joy. Wise choices will watch over you. Understanding will keep you safe. (Proverbs 2:1–2, 9–11)

Moses acknowledged that truth was our best friend when he challenged the nation of Israel with these words:

Now, Israel, what does the LORD your God require from you, but to fear the LORD your God, to walk in all His ways and love Him, and to serve the LORD your God with all your heart and with all your soul, and to keep the LORD's commandments and His statutes which I am commanding you today for your good? (Deuteronomy 10:12–13 NASB, emphasis added)

Every truth, every rule, and every guideline coming from God's Word is issued from the loving heart and character of God for our own good. "I know the plans I have for you," God told the nation of Israel. "They are plans for good and not for disaster, to give you a future and a hope" (Jeremiah 29:11). He went on to express his desire for his children to have "one heart and one purpose: to worship me forever, for their own good and for the good of all their descendents" (Jeremiah 32:39). These two passages in Jeremiah were spoken to the nation of Israel, but the truth they express remains today—God seeks the good of his people, and his laws are part of that protection and provision. The late apologist and author Ron Carlson used to speak of the Ten Commandments as the "Ten Great Freedoms." A nation that embraces and follows God's laws would find that instead of its freedom being limited, it would have true freedom and great liberty. For example, if a nation of people follow the eighth commandment—"You shall not steal"—they would have no reason to lock doors or worry about robbers.

Truth is our best friend, and it is an inseparable part of what real love is. While cultural tolerance may disguise itself as caring, understanding, and loving, it lacks the moral authority of an authentic love that looks out for the best interest of others. That is another quality of authentic, real love—it is always other-focused.

REAL LOVE IS OTHER-FOCUSED

Being other-focused does not come naturally. You don't have to be very observant to recognize that from infancy we all inherited a self-centered nature. The quality of loving others unselfishly comes from God. When scripture says, "God is love" (1 John 4:16), it means more than "God loves us." He is the very meaning and essence of what a loving relationship is all about. He is both our model and source of real love. And this is true because God is triune—meaning there is one God who eternally exists as three persons: Father, Son, and Holy Spirit. Thus, God is *inherently* a relational being who created us to be in relationship with him and with others (Mark 12:28–31).

Created in God's image, we were meant to love both him and others as he loves. He loves perfectly, and he wants to teach us how to love in a healthy way. Jesus said, "Just as I have loved you, you should love each other" (John 13:34).

God's kind of love is unique. The apostle Paul gives a good description of what love does and does not do. "Love is patient and kind. Love is not jealous or boastful or proud or rude. It does not demand its own way. It is not irritable, and it keeps no record of being wronged. It does not rejoice about injustice but rejoices whenever the truth wins out" (1 Corinthians 13:4–6).

Paul also wrote that "love does no wrong to others" (Romans

13:10). Instead, we are to treat all people as we would like to be treated. Remember the Golden Rule? "Do to others whatever you would like them to do to you" (Matthew 7:12). Paul put it this way: "In humility value others above yourselves, not looking to your own interests but each of you to the interests of the others" (Philippians 2:3–4 NIV).

When Jesus was asked to identify the most important commandment, he said it was to (1) love God, and (2) "love your neighbor as yourself" (Matthew 22:39). Paul gave us a specific application of this principle when he told husbands "to love their wives as they love their own bodies. . . . No one hates his own body but feeds and cares for it" (Ephesians 5:28–29).

The predominant quality of this Godlike love is that it is other-focused. "This is real love," scripture states, "not that we loved God, but that he loved us and sent his Son as a sacrifice to take away our sins" (1 John 4:10). Jesus wasn't looking out for his personal interest when he entered our world to die for us. He was focused on us and what we needed. That is what true love does.

As we can see by these abundant scriptures, true love is other-focused. But the question remains, how do we exercise true love while at the same time disagreeing with a person's wrong choices about morality and truth? How do we blend real love with traditional tolerance that looks beyond the faults and failures of others and still loves them for who they are? How do we define that kind of love?

DEFINING REAL LOVE

Drawing from the scriptures quoted earlier and others that are similar, we can derive a concise definition of God's kind of love—real love:

Love is making the security, happiness, and welfare of another person as important as your own.

This kind of love, authentic love, protects the loved one from harm and provides for his or her good. Biblical love is not merely focused on another but on the *good* of another, even if the other does not recognize or accept the reality of the good. Love recognizes that there is an order to the goods it affirms and denies that the order is outside the experience or judgment of the other. When two people exercise this kind of love in a relationship, each looks to provide for the other's best and protect the other from the worst, regardless of how they feel. Because its priority is seeking the best interest of the loved one, real love will not do things that are harmful to the security, happiness, and welfare of another person. Even though Renee may *feel* that sleeping with her boyfriend is loving, doing so does not provide for his security, happiness, and welfare and thus does not qualify as an act of love.[2]

Why is Kenton upset that his daughter is sleeping with her boyfriend? Is it merely because it violates the moral values he tried to teach his daughter? Is it because it may somehow embarrass him or reflect badly on his standing with his Christian friends or the church? That should not be Kenton's primary concern. His primary concern should be his daughter's best interest. When he makes his daughter's security, happiness, and welfare as important to him as his own, it focuses his attention on how Renee's improper behavior can negatively affect her physically, spiritually, emotionally, and relationally.

Teri is concerned about alienating her daughter if she and Kenton come across as too harsh. That is a valid concern. But her tolerant attitude toward immorality that essentially says, "Do what *you* think is best, dear," isn't looking out for Renee's best interest either. Endorsing an attitude or action that is harmful to another person does, in the long run, not truly love. Real love—God's kind of love—seeks to protect a loved one from harm and provide for her best interest.

PROVIDE AND PROTECT: THE NATURE OF REAL LOVE

I (Sean) have three children. Like any good parent, I have said things like, "Shane, don't touch the stove"; "Shauna, look both ways before you cross the street"; and "Come on, Scottie, eat those vegetables." I don't issue those directives merely because they are the rules of the Stephanie and Sean household. My wife and I have not placed restrictions or boundaries on our children to spoil their fun or make them miserable. Loving parents impose rules to protect their children and to provide for them.

God has issued his commands to us out of these same two very powerful positive motivations—to provide for us and to protect us. He has given clear instructions related to our sexual behavior— "Flee from sexual immorality" (1 Corinthians 6:18 NIV); "Husbands, love your wives" (Colossians 3:19); "You shall not commit adultery" (Exodus 20:14 NIV)—and a variety of others. He didn't give these instructions to limit or restrict us, but to protect us from harm and provide for our best interest. That is what other-focused love does.

Scripture directs husbands to apply this other-focused, provide-and-protect kind of love when the apostle Paul tells them "to love their own wives as their own bodies. He who loves his own wife loves himself; for no one ever hated his own flesh, but nourishes and cherishes it, just as Christ also does the church" (Ephesians 5:28–29 NASB).

The apostle's use of the words *nourish* and *cherish* here is not by mere happenstance. It clearly helps us to see how we are to make the security, happiness, and welfare of another as important to us as our own. Just as we are careful to nourish and cherish our own bodies, we are to nourish and cherish others in love.

To *nourish* means to provide for and bring to maturity. It means to care for and contribute to the whole person—relationally, physically, spiritually, and socially. Love is a provider. It requires that we provide for the security, happiness, and welfare of others—just as we provide for our own—in order to bring them to maturity.

To *cherish* means to protect from the elements. Imagine a nest of newborn eaglets high on a mountain crag, exposed to the sky. An angry thunderstorm is rolling in. The mother eagle swoops down to the nest and spreads her wings over the eaglets to protect them from the pounding rain and swirling wind. That's a picture of what it means to cherish.

Ephesians 5:29 tells us that it is natural for us to cherish ourselves—that is, to protect ourselves from anything that may endanger our mental, physical, spiritual, or social well-being. We buckle up and drive safely to prevent physical injury or death on the highway. We monitor our sugar and calorie intake to keep our bodies healthy. In other words, we love ourselves enough to protect ourselves from harm. Love is a protector as well as a provider.

For a husband to love his wife as he loves himself means he does whatever he can to *provide for* (nourish) the security, happiness, and welfare of his wife relationally, physically, spiritually, and socially, just as he would provide for himself. And he is to *protect* (cherish) his wife from anything that might hinder her from achieving maturity, just as he would protect himself.

By understanding that real love provides and protects another person, we gain insight as to why love makes a sexual relationship right.

WHY LOVE MAKES A SEXUAL RELATIONSHIP RIGHT

Renee's justification for sleeping with her boyfriend was that it was right for them because they "loved each other." In other words, "love makes it right." It seems that Teri, her mother, may have been influenced by that kind of thinking as well.

I (Josh) shock parents and church leaders when I say that I agree, in a way, with today's young people—I believe that true love *does* make it right. You may have already come to that conclusion yourself, because when true love is founded on the biblical standard for sex, it waits to have sex within the context it was meant to be expressed in—marriage. If Tony truly loved Renee and Renee truly loved Tony, they would wait to engage in sex until they committed to each other in marriage. The truth is, the physical, spiritual, and relational security, happiness, and welfare of both of them is best achieved by waiting.

True love commits wholeheartedly. As we noted above, it commits to cherishing, protecting, and providing—all of which are self-sacrificing activities that place the other's welfare above one's own. When two lovers marry, they are making a public vow committing to provide for and protect each other through thick or thin. That kind of committed love compels a couple to wait to engage in sex until after marriage—which is the context in which love makes it right.

When it comes to the matter of our sexual morality, God, in his love, wants to provide for us and protect us. It's this simple: when we and our children honor God's boundaries and prohibitions for sexual behavior, we benefit. Obedience to his negative commands to avoid sexual immorality offers a very positive result.

In biblical terms, sexual immorality is all sex that occurs outside of a marriage between one man and one woman (extramarital and premarital sex). Scripture gives the following guidelines:

- *You must abstain from. . .sexual immorality.* (Acts 15:29)
- *Run from sexual sin!* (1 Corinthians 6:18)
- *We must not engage in sexual immorality.* (1 Corinthians 10:8)
- *Among you there must not be even a hint of sexual immorality. . .because these are improper for God's holy people.* (Ephesians 5:3, NIV)
- *God's will is for you to be holy, so stay away from all sexual sin.* (1 Thessalonians 4:3)

Respecting the boundaries of sexual morality and prohibitions for extramarital and premarital sex does bring protection and provision. Here are just a few ways it does this:

Protection from	Provision for
guilt	freedom
unplanned pregnancy	optimum atmosphere for child raising
sexually transmitted diseases	peace of mind
sexual insecurity	trust
emotional distress	true intimacy

Experiencing these benefits can definitely maximize a person's sex life in marriage. For example, I (Sean) made a clear choice to wait until I made the loving commitment of marriage before experiencing sexual relations. That commitment meant I would remain sexually celibate until I met and married my high school sweetheart (Stephanie) and then remain faithful to her. Stephanie made that same commitment. And because we both were obedient to God's commands regarding sex, we have been protected from feelings of guilt and have enjoyed a consistent relationship with each other.

We never had to go through the heartache of a pregnancy before marriage. Consequently, we have not experienced the heart-wrenching ordeal of planning an adoption or struggling with getting married before we were ready.

We have been protected from the fear that any sexually transmitted disease might come into our marriage bed.

We have been protected from the sexual insecurity that can come from being compared to past sexual lovers one's spouse may have had. And consequently, we have experienced the provision of trust in our relationship.

We have been protected from the emotional distress that premarital sex can bring and the feelings of betrayal that an extra-marital affair can cause. As a result, we have enjoyed relational intimacy together unobstructed by breaches of trust or ghosts from the past. And even more than avoidance of these negative consequences, obedience has helped bring an atmosphere of joy, freedom, life, and happiness that God desires each of us to experience. I don't want to portray our relationship in a Pollyannaish manner as if we don't have any struggles. Like every other couple, of course we do. But this is an area where following God's commandments has benefited us immensely—more than we ever could have imagined when we were younger.

Sex as God designed it is meant to be lived within the context of healthy boundaries—prohibitions before marriage and fidelity after marriage. Following God's design allows a couple to experience the beauty of sex as it was meant to be experienced. But it is vitally important that we know—and that our children understand—what these boundaries are and be able to identify them by name. Because it is these boundaries and limits that make "no" such a positive answer—and when we live within them, they are the very means by which sex is maximized. Take time to instill the boundaries God has given us to maximize the joy he wants us to experience in our sex lives. Let your children know how purity and faithfulness are their best friends when it comes to finding the most joy in sexuality.

The Boundary of Purity

The Bible says, "Marriage should be honored by all, and the marriage bed kept pure" (Hebrews 13:4 NIV). "God's will is for you to be holy, so stay away from all sexual sin. Then each of you will control his own body and live in holiness and honor—not in lustful passion. . . . God has called us to live holy lives, not impure lives" (1 Thessalonians 4:3–5, 7). Purity is God's boundary that provides for a maximum sex life and protects us from the negative consequences of sexual immorality.

What does it mean to be pure? Have you ever had a candy bar that identified itself on the wrapper as "pure milk chocolate"? What about a jar of honey? Some labels read: "Pure honey—no artificial sweeteners." *Pure* describing chocolate or honey means there is no foreign substance to contaminate it or to keep it from being and tasting like authentic chocolate or real honey.

To be pure sexually is to "live according to God's original design," without allowing anything to come in to ruin his ideal plan for sex. While God desires that some be single (1 Corinthians 7), sex was designed to be experienced between one man (husband)

and one woman (wife) in a lifelong committed marital relationship. To actually have more than one sexual partner, or to look at pornography and even *think* about another sex partner, would be to bring a foreign substance into the relationship, and thus introduce a kind of impurity. If you were to drop a dirty pebble into a glass of pure water, it would become adulterated—impure. A glass of water without any impurities in it is an unadulterated glass of water. God wants us to have sex lives—in both body and mind—that are unadulterated.

Our young people need to know that God designed sex to be experienced within an unbroken circle, a pure union between two virgins entering into an exclusive relationship. That pure union can be broken even *before* marriage if one or both of the partners has not kept the marriage bed pure by waiting to have sex until it can be done in the purity of a husband-wife relationship.

Where did sexual purity come from? From the very character of God himself. God says, "Be holy, for I am holy" (1 Peter 1:16 NASB). "All who have this hope [of being like Christ when he returns] in him purify themselves, just as he [Christ] is pure" (1 John 3:3 NIV). God by nature is holy and pure. "There is no evil in him" (Psalm 92:15). What Kenton and Teri want to help Renee understand is that if she remains sexually pure before and after marriage—in both body and heart—she and her boyfriend, Tony, will enjoy the protection and provision of sex and experience it as God meant it to be experienced. That is what all our young people need to understand.

And if young people have made mistakes already, they need to understand that God forgives them. The reason Jesus came is to forgive fallen people and to remove their sin. If marriage illustrates Christ's relationship to the church, sexual impurity represents unfaithfulness to God, and we have *all* been unfaithful and impure to varying degrees. Ultimately, our need for purity (in all areas of life) is satisfied in Christ because he is the only one who lived a perfectly holy life (John 8:46). According to 1 John 1:9, "If we confess our sins to him, he is faithful and just to forgive us our sins and to cleanse us from all wickedness."

The Boundary of Faithfulness

The seventh commandment is, "You must not commit adultery" (Exodus 20:14). Jesus made the point that once a man and woman are united as one in marriage, they are not to commit adultery but remain faithful to one another. He said, "Let no one split apart what God has joined together" (Mark 10:9). God told Israel, "I hate divorce! . . . So guard your heart; do not be unfaithful to your wife" (Malachi 2:16).

What couples do at their wedding is commit to be faithful to one another—"to have and to hold from this day forward: for better, for worse; for richer, for poorer; in sickness and in health; to love and to cherish till death do us part. And hereto I pledge you my faithfulness." Perhaps nothing is more rewarding than to sense that someone loves you more than any other and will devote himself or herself to you for life.

I (Josh) have traveled away from home for most of my married life. I have had more than one opportunity to be unfaithful to Dottie. But in over forty years of marriage, by God's grace I have resisted temptation and demonstrated loyalty, faithfulness, and devoted commitment to only one love-and-sex relationship in my life. And that, of course, is my relationship with Dottie. That commitment means the world to her. It deepens her sense of worth, and it gives her security and tells her she is loved. Of all the billions of women on this planet, she is the one and only lover for me.

God created us with the desire and longing to be that "one and only" to someone else. That desire came directly from the very nature of God himself. "Understand. . .that the LORD your God is indeed God," Moses told the Israelites. "He is the faithful God who keeps his covenant for a thousand generations" (Deuteronomy 7:9).

Countering the influence that cultural tolerance has had on our young people's understanding of sexual morality isn't necessarily easy. We need to take time to intentionally instill God's design for sex. Correcting the distorted view our young people may have about love and sex involves imparting a clear understanding of who God is, who we are in relationship to him, and how he has given us a way of relating to one another and a model for doing it. This biblical narrative about God and his truth is about a way of living and thinking that must be incrementally and consistently imparted to our children. God's instructions for instilling the truth of scripture into young people are as fitting for us today as they were when he first gave them to Israelite parents: "Repeat them again and again to your children. Talk about them when you are at home and when you are on the road, when you are going to bed and when you are getting up" (Deuteronomy 6:7).

Here are a few examples of situations that you can use as times to convey God's boundaries for a maximum sex life.

- *Celebrate anniversaries.* Wedding anniversaries are ideal times to let your children and their friends know how faithfulness and purity are God's plan to protect and provide for us in our relationships. This can include people who have suffered divorce but are now pursuing a faithful relationship and oneness in their marriage. Make your own anniversary a family celebration. Let your children know how much marital fidelity means to you. Explain what the marriage commitment has done for your relationship. The more that members of your own family see how faithfulness and purity have benefited your lives, the greater the impact it will have on them.

Don't underestimate the ability of younger children (six, five, or four years old, for example) to understand the principles of sexual purity and marital fidelity. You have an excellent opportunity to build a foundation for their sexual chastity by helping them understand the principles of faithfulness and purity. You can explain to them your faithfulness to your spouse by putting it in the form of promise keeping. "I promised I would love your mother always, and that's what I am going to do because I love your mother more than anyone, and God would be disappointed in me if I broke my promise to her." You can explain marital fidelity to young children by saying, "I live only with your father and with no one else because I love him so much and because God created a wife to love only one man in that way." Teach them early of your commitment to each other and how you are exclusively devoted to each other.

Pastors and youth workers, you can take advantage of your anniversary or that of a mature couple in your church. Have your spouse come into the youth group or adult small group for a faithfulness and purity celebration. Explain how those principles have brought provision and protection into the marriage.

- *Take full advantage of weddings.* Whether you are a youth worker, pastor, or parent, you can use a wedding to celebrate God's principle of faithfulness and purity. Make sure your children understand its significance. Take time prior to and following the ceremony to emphasize the commitment the couple is making and their promise to be faithful for a lifetime. Get a copy of the marriage vows and read them together with your younger children. Some teenagers find it a bit stuffy or unconventional to read the vows together, but you can at least make it meaningful to a child or preteen. Weddings are an ideal time to reinforce God's way of love and sex within the marriage commitment—and how that reflects the relational character of God.

- *Use opportunities presented by TV, news, and current affairs.* Take advantage of some of the many opportunities to correct the warped portrayals of love and sex in the "entertainment" media and news or to highlight those that are positive. When you and your children, for example, see something on television or in the movies that contradicts God's standard for sex, discuss the benefits of obeying God's commands and the consequences of violating them. You may be surprised how insightful young people are in detecting the benefits and consequences of people's actions once they begin to see life through the biblical narrative about truth concerning love and sex.[3]

An expression of authentic love honors the boundaries of purity and faithfulness. That kind of loving prompts us to provide for another's best and protect him or her from harm. Kenton aims to portray that kind of love for his daughter, although he may express it imperfectly. His wife, Teri, needs to understand that loving her daughter isn't about agreeing with her in an attempt to prevent alienation. She needs to point her daughter to the truth about love and sex, knowing that obedience to God's negative commands gives us the best chance to experience God's design for relationships. Endorsing immoral behavior is not equivalent to loving a person, nor is correcting that behavior equivalent to rejecting a person.

Proponents of cultural tolerance, however, will point out that when you fail to endorse a person's beliefs and behavior, you are, in effect, rejecting the person. Many claim that homosexuality is not merely a sexual act or a natural orientation; it is a state of being— an identity. Many assert that people are born gay, and when you condemn homosexuality, it's an affront to their personhood and a direct condemnation and discrimination against them as human beings.

What so offended Chad was that his dad, Todd, was in effect (in his opinion) condemning his friend's brother. When Todd said, "Homosexuality is wrong, and we shouldn't be celebrating it," that, in Chad's mind, was an outright rejection of a person. And if being gay is an identity, how can Todd or any of us lovingly accept the person without approving of choices he or she may make?

Granted, that is a tough question, and because many Christians have failed to address it adequately, the culture has answered it for us. That answer hasn't been a pretty one. When the Christian community declares homosexuality to be wrong, sinful, or unnatural, they are labeled intolerant, bigoted, hateful, and unloving. Claiming,

"We love the sinner; we just hate the sin" doesn't cut it with this culture. In fact, that phrase is offensive to a generation steeped in cultural tolerance. And the statement is far too simplistic. Our own churched young people, for the most part, defend their gay friends and say we as Christians should accept them for who they are—which often means endorsing certain behaviors we find objectionable.

We are here to humbly offer a solution to this dilemma. There is a way to love people for who they are while at the same time not endorsing their behavior. Jesus teaches us how authentic love does just that. Real love means loving people where they are regardless of what they do. That is what true love does. We will unpack the real meaning and application of true love in the next chapter.

CHAPTER 6

TRUE LOVE

Hours had passed since Chad stormed out the door, infuriated with his father, Todd. Chad was now home again, so Todd made his way up to his son's room in an attempt to smooth things over.

"Can we talk?" Todd asked as he poked his head into Chad's room.

"I don't want to fight with you, Dad."

"I don't want to fight either. I just want you to know I don't hate your friend's brother or anyone else."

Todd entered the room and sat on the edge of the bed. Chad nodded slightly as he closed his laptop. "I know you don't hate people, Dad. I was just really angry when I said those things."

"I know," Todd responded reassuringly. "But I want you to know I don't hate gay people." Chad looked at his dad but said nothing.

"All I'm trying to say," Todd continued, "is that there are certain things that are wrong, and I'm sorry that you're offended because I believe what I believe."

"But your beliefs are causing you to reject a person for being who he is."

"I'm not rejecting anyone. I'm just standing up for what's right and pointing out what's wrong—and son, whether you agree with it or not, homosexuality is wrong."

"Because you believe that doesn't make it wrong for everyone," Chad stated firmly. "And when you say the people at the gay games are wrong, you are rejecting them big-time. You are putting them down as human beings and—"

"I'm not putting them down," Todd interrupted.

"You are, too," Chad countered. "Being gay is who Mike's brother is—he didn't choose to be gay; he was just born that way. And you are making him out like he's a pervert or something."

"Well, homosexuality is sinful, son. It's not the way God

designed us—it's unnatural."

"Can you hear yourself, Dad?" Chad countered as he shook his head in disapproval. "You have no right to judge like that. You've got to accept people for who they are."

BORN WHAT WAY?

Chad and most in our culture believe the Christian community is being judgmental by condemning the sexual practices of people who were born with a predisposition toward the same sex. By and large, our culture has accepted the idea that gays are "born that way" and Christians are intolerant of a natural behavior. We are being conditioned to think that people who are gay have no choice; they are simply being who they were born to be.

This is faulty thinking on at least two levels. First, in spite of what you see and read in the media, scientific research has not established that homosexuality has a biological basis. Second, even if it did, that wouldn't mean a genetic disposition toward a behavior makes it right.

But if homosexuality isn't hardwired within individuals, how is it that our young people and the culture have come to accept the claim that it is? In the early 1990s, two Harvard-trained scientists released studies that led the media and the public to believe homosexuality was both innate and immutable. The studies did not say that, but they were interpreted to mean that homosexuality was both natural and inherent, fixed and unchanging.

In 1991 neurobiologist Simon LeVay reported that the hypothalamus, a structure in the brain, is smaller in homosexuals than in heterosexuals.[1] Then in 1993 geneticist Dean Hamer published his research claiming that homosexuality has a genetic origin.[2] Together these studies led many people to conclude that homosexuality has a biogenetic cause, with the direct inference that individuals are born gay.

When scientists began questioning such conclusions, both LeVay and Hamer clarified their findings. "It's important to stress what I didn't find," wrote LeVay. "I did not prove that homosexuality is genetic, or find a genetic cause for being gay. I didn't show that gay men are 'born that way,' the most common mistake people make in interpreting my work."[3]

Dean Hamer later conceded, "Sexual identification is more a matter of environment than heredity."[4] And when pressed as to whether homosexuality was based solely in biology, Hamer replied emphatically, "Absolutely not."[5] Even the American Psychological Association now acknowledges there is no scientific basis for concluding that people are born gay. They say in their brochure on sexual orientation and homosexuality: "There is no consensus among scientists about the exact reasons that an individual develops a heterosexual, bisexual, gay, or lesbian orientation. Although much research has examined the possible genetic, hormonal, developmental, social, and cultural influences on sexual orientation, no findings have emerged that permit scientists to conclude that sexual orientation is determined by any particular factor or factors."[6]

Even if it could be proven that there is a "gay gene" and people were born with a homosexual predisposition, would that make homosexual behavior or same-sex marriage okay? If so, then many other orientations and behaviors should be judged on the same basis—behaviors such as alcohol addiction, gambling addiction, and according to some, even unfaithfulness and sexual promiscuity. Researchers at the State University of New York at Binghamton have discovered that about half of all people have a gene that makes them predisposed to certain behaviors. According to lead researcher, Dr. Justin Garcia, people with the DRD4 gene are "more likely to have a history of uncommitted sex, including one-night stands and acts of infidelity," and this gene is "also responsible for alcohol and gambling addictions."[7] So does that mean half of all people are headed in the wrong direction from birth?

Actually, it is even worse than that. According to scripture, we were all born headed in the wrong direction. "When Adam sinned, sin entered the world. Adam's sin brought death, so death spread to everyone, for everyone sinned" (Romans 5:12). Whether we are genetically more prone to be unfaithful or addicted to alcohol or other misbehaviors, the point is, every one of us sins and has a predisposition to keep on sinning. Every one of us is drawn to certain activities that are harmful but extremely hard to resist.

The question is, does the ingrained presence of virtually irresistible behaviors justify those behaviors? After all, if we are addicted sinners, then can't we just claim we are doing what we were born to do? If being a sinner does justify certain behaviors, the young woman standing on Sunset Boulevard in Hollywood could say, "Hey, don't judge me. I have the DRD4 gene, so I was born to be a prostitute. You are being intolerant and bigoted to call me a sinner, for I'm just being who I was born to be." And what about the man who has gambled away all his money, is deep in debt, and has left his wife and children without house or home? "Come on, don't condemn me," he could plead. "I'm an addicted gambler by birth. This is who I am. It's my identity. So when you speak against my gambling habit, you are rejecting me as a person."

It's natural to look for excuses when people accuse us of doing something wrong. We all might like to say, "Don't blame me; my sin gene made me do it." While scripture teaches that we were all born sinners, committing wrong is largely about choosing to do wrong. Strictly from a theological perspective, it's true we are all slaves to sin (Romans 7:14) and in need of God's grace to turn away from wrong behavior. But we were created with a will—we all have a choice. Some may have a harder choice to make because of certain genes (nature) or because of their difficult environment (nurture). But we are still responsible for our behavior and choices. Wise Solomon wrote that all of us will be held accountable "for everything we do, including every secret thing, whether good or bad" (Ecclesiastes 12:14). The apostle Paul agreed, saying that, "we are each responsible for our own conduct" (Galatians 6:5). While it's true that our choices take us down certain paths in life, they don't define our value as created beings by God.

GENES AND ACTIONS DO NOT DEFINE WHO WE WERE CREATED TO BE

Chad claimed that his father was judgmental and that he was rejecting Mike's gay brother because of who he was. Chad, like most people in our culture, has bought into the fallacy that our genetic disposition, our actions, and our lifestyle define who we are.

Cultural tolerance and its narrative about the truth of who we are as individuals allow no differentiation between who a person is and that person's beliefs, behavior, or lifestyle. If it were written as an equation, it would look like this:

Who I Am = What I Do

Based on this narrative, who you are is inseparable from what you do and think and believe; your identity is wrapped up in your conduct. It stands to reason, then, if people express any disagreement with your beliefs, they are disparaging *you*. If others say that your behavior is wrong, they are judging you. When your actions are criticized, you are being criticized. If people can't accept the validity of your lifestyle, then they are being intolerant of you.

From the vantage point of this concept of personhood, you can understand how today's culture would hear the assertion that homosexual behavior is sinful as "God hates gays." Disparage what people do and in their minds you reject the essence of an individual's personhood. Hate the sin of homosexuality and gays will tend to feel you hate their very being.

This entire line of thinking leads the culture to believe that accepting a person for who that person is must include approving and endorsing what that person believes or does. Anything short of that is seen as a rejection of the person, as well as judgmental and intolerant.

The entire premise of that type of thinking is wrong. We are not what we do. Our genetic disposition or how we behave does not define who God created us to be. God created humans in his image, which gives them immense dignity and worth. We were meant to live in relationship with God and with our fellow human beings. He gave us a world to care for and enjoy (Genesis 2:15). We inherited his ability to love and communicate our thoughts, intents, and feelings to others. He imparted to us a sense of value for life and human relationships, as well as satisfaction and joy in accomplishing things that honor him. He also honored us with the charge to be masters over all life (see Genesis 1:26).

Although sin has separated us from God, his original intent for us and the reality that we were created in his image have not changed. What we do or don't do may distort that image, but our worth to God as human beings never changes.

TRUE LOVE SEPARATES DOING FROM BEING

The biblical narrative on love of others is altogether different from that of today's culture. Jesus said, "A new commandment I give to you, that you love one another: just as I have loved you, you also are to love one another" (John 13:34 ESV). So how has Christ loved you? He values all people for their inherent worth and offers grace freely to all people without exception. Cultural tolerance, on the other hand, claims to accept everyone's differing beliefs, values, and lifestyles, yet it qualifies that acceptance. For example, anyone who believes in a universal truth is rejected outright.

What distinguishes God's unconditional acceptance from that of our culture is authentic love. His love is intended to make the security, happiness, and welfare of another as important as his own. It is other-focused, not performance-focused. God knows the real truth about us—that we were created in his image—and that truth allows him to separate the person from performance. God unconditionally values us for who we are without always approving of what we do, because he separates the value of the person from the acts of the person.

Real valuing of another's personhood expressed in the context of authentic love separates doing from being and sees the acts of sin distinct from the sinner (which, by the way, is *all* of us). But that doesn't take the sinner off the hook for his or her sin. The biblical narrative of truth tells us God created us to be relational— he shaped our natures to enjoy a relationship with him. While the first created couple chose not to trust God, no amount of sin could destroy the reality of their innate status as God's children. Yet that status did not keep God from recognizing and addressing their sin.

This is where the balance of truth and traditional tolerance is perfectly played out through God's response to the human choice to sin. Although he dearly loves the sinner, sin is too big an issue to ignore. He can't just say, "Hey, all humans mess up and do wrong. But because I love them, I'll just forget those sins." God's absolute holiness keeps him from doing that. He simply can't accept sin. The Bible says of him, "Your eyes are too pure to look on evil; you cannot tolerate wrongdoing" (Habakkuk 1:13 NIV). He is so holy that he "cannot allow sin in any form" (Habakkuk 1:13 TLB). God's holy response to sin is repulsion. There is beauty to his intolerance because he is heartsick at what sin has done to his created humans. So in compassion he offers mercy.

God can respond with such grace toward us, even in our sin, because he sees a distinction between our "essence" and our "nature." Our essence is that we are beings created in his image with great dignity and worth. Our nature is malignantly infected because of sin. He actually views the condition of sinfulness separate from the essence of who we are as his lost children. The Bible says that "your iniquities have separated you from your God" (Isaiah 59:2 NIV). Isaiah makes a clear separation between us as God's lost children, created in his image, and what we do—sin. It is clear that what we do is *not* the same as who we are. If that were the case, God couldn't remove "our sins as far away from us as the east is from the west" (Psalm 103:12 TLB). He cannot remove us from our essence, but by his grace through Christ he can transform our nature.

Even though God makes a distinction between who we are and what we have done, actions have consequences. As we have said, our sin has resulted in God's wrath and death—a separation from the holy God (Romans 6:23). What's worse, we can't do anything to reverse our death sentence. We are doomed (Ephesians 2:1), and we can't even earn points with God "based on our good deeds" (Romans 3:27 TLB). God may love us for who we are, but he can't accept the sin that has infected us with a death sentence. And that is when Christ's authentic love steps in and takes action.

Even though God's holiness cannot embrace our infected life of sin, he freely offers humans salvation because of his love (John 3:16–21). So despite our sinfulness, he offers us grace. And it is that grace—favor that is not merited—that cost him dearly.

In effect God says, "You are my child, created in my image. That is who you are. Your misbehavior is wrong. My holiness cannot overlook that. In fact, I hate what it has done to you—it has separated you from me. So my love compels me to sacrifice my only Son and allow him to endure a cruel death on the cross. This satisfies the requirement of both my holiness and justice. And if you will accept my Son's death as yours, his sacrifice will atone for your sins. I then can forgive you and transform you from death to life. Because I can see you through the lens of Christ's sacrifice, I can remove the curse of sin from you. Then you will no longer be my lost and dead child, but my found child who will be alive in relationship with me."

God's undeserved love and acceptance through the sacrifice of Christ and imputation of his righteousness to our account is able to remove our sins and restore each of us as individuals created in his image with great dignity and worth. And more than anything, he wants us to be free of a life of wrongdoing so we can know God personally and enjoy him (John 17:1–5).

God's love is about our best interest and bringing us joy in him. Jesus said, "I have told you this so that my joy may be in you and that your joy may be complete" (John 15:11 NIV). He knows our sinful behavior leads us to an unsatisfying, joy-sapped life. The reason he wants us to follow his commands and live consistently with what is moral and right is because doing so will result in our happiness and give our life meaning (John 10:10), and restore us to himself—the ultimate source of goodness, truth, and beauty.

That is the kind of love and acceptance Renee's parents wished they could express to her, but their attempt fell short. It's the kind of love and acceptance Todd wanted to demonstrate toward Mike's brother but failed to articulate clearly. It's the kind of love and acceptance you no doubt want to demonstrate to your children and the world around you. It is certainly what most people want and seek. But that kind of love and acceptance isn't necessarily easy for us to grasp and express. Many of us haven't seen that kind of expression up close and personal in our family of origin or perhaps even in a present relationship. Yet Jesus is a perfect model of that kind of accepting love. As we look to him as our example, we can gain insight into how we can love others as he loves us.

AN EXAMPLE OF TRUE LOVE

Scripture tells us that we are to love others as Christ loved us (John 13:34–35). As we have discovered, that isn't a "normal" kind of love. To help get a clearer picture of how Christ accepts others without approving of their lifestyle, let's look at John 4, where Jesus meets a woman at a public well. Scripture says Jesus "left Judea and returned to Galilee. He had to go through Samaria on the way" (John 4:3–4). Jesus' travel itinerary is the first indicator of how loving he is.

The reality was, Jesus didn't *have to go* through Samaria to get to Galilee. The "devoted" Jews of the day would never go through Samaria to get to Galilee from Judea. Galilee was due north of Judea, and Samaria was right in the middle between the two. But a Jewish person would either travel around that region by going east to Jericho then following the Jordan Valley north, or would travel by boat west of the Samaritan area via the Mediterranean Sea. Whatever the case, a strict Jewish person would consider the out-of-the-way journey well worth it to avoid running into a Samaritan.

Jews tried to avoid Samaritans because Samaria had a long history of tension with Judea. In Jesus' day, Jews considered Samaritans "half-breeds" and wanted nothing to do with them. Additionally, Jews were outraged that the Samaritans had tampered with scripture to change the place of worship from Jerusalem to Mount Gerizim. In effect, Jews considered Samaritans heretics. So a true follower of Judaism would not dignify the Samaritans—or pollute himself or herself—by even walking on their soil.

Obviously, Jesus' feelings toward the Samaritans were different. He made his journey right through the middle of Samaria until he came to Sychar, "and Jesus, tired from the long walk, sat wearily beside the well [Jacob's well] about noontime" (John 4:6).

Samaria was an arid land, and water was a precious commodity. People would come to this well in the cool of evening or in the morning before the day heated up. Few would come at noontime. Anyone foolish enough to be drawing water at this time of day was probably trying to avoid being seen by the townspeople.

Jesus was sitting alone by the well, waiting for his disciples who had gone into town to buy food. Then along came a Samaritan woman. Not expecting to see anyone, she probably began to draw water and didn't even notice Jesus. She was suddenly startled when a masculine voice behind her said, "Please give me a drink" (verse 7).

The woman's response is significant: "You are a Jew, and I am a Samaritan woman. Why are you asking me for a drink?" (verse 9). This woman was shocked on two levels. First, this was a *man* who was talking to her. It was highly unusual for a Jewish man to speak to an unfamiliar woman. To do so was considered shameful, illicit, and in some cases, even scandalous. Notice that later in verse 27 when the disciples showed up, "They were shocked to find him talking to a woman, but none of them had the nerve to ask, 'What do you want with her?'" In that day, men with good intentions didn't talk to women who were strangers.

The second indicator of Jesus' love was that Jewish men or women simply didn't converse with the heretical Samaritans. It's clear that the woman was taken aback by the very fact that he spoke to her. She might have thought, *He's one of those who thinks we're scum for just being who we are. His people condemn us for our lifestyle. But on the other hand, he doesn't seem to be doing that. What is it with this guy?*

Jesus' noncondemning attitude was not the only thing that took her off guard. To add to her wonder, he actually asked her for help. He was thirsty, and he asked *her* if she would give him some of her water.

It's one thing to love someone whose behavior or lifestyle you find morally offensive. It's quite another thing to go so far as asking that person for some kind of help. That almost sounds like befriending a person with an objectionable lifestyle, doesn't it? Might Christlike love even lead a Christian who is opposed to homosexual behavior to become friends with a gay person? Of course!

I (Sean) know Christians who say, "Hey, I would have no problem befriending a gay person." But many who respond that way probably often don't currently have a friend who is gay. It is one thing to say theoretically that we have no problem befriending gay people; it is another thing to actually build that relationship. I regularly interact with people who are gay, and some of them have become my friends. I have been blessed by these relationships, as I have with many of my other friendships. And I trust they have been blessed as well. Your children very likely have friends who are gay. We may grasp the idea of what Christlike acceptance means on a conceptual level, but until we build genuine relationships with people who are gay—and see them as equal image bearers—we will continue to hold unhealthy and false stereotypes.

Now, back to Jesus' interaction with the Samaritan woman.

After he asked the woman for a drink, notice what he said: "If you only knew the gift God has for you and who you are speaking to, you would ask me, and I would give you living water" (verse 10).

Now he really had this woman confused. Not only did this man consider her worth talking to—even to the extent of seeking her help for a drink of water—but he also offered her an extraordinary gift. She knew the difference between "dead" and "living" water. Living water referred to moving water, such as a fresh river or spring. Dead water was standing or stored water. Samaria had no rivers, so Jesus' statement was confusing. Jacob had dug a well there because there was no river or stream. So how could this man be offering her fresh, superior water?

But naturally, if he could deliver on the fresh water, she was up for it. "Please sir," the woman said, "give me this water! Then I'll never be thirsty again, and I won't have to come here to get water" (verse 15).

Then Jesus throws her a big curve. "Go and get your husband" (verse 16). Of course he knew she had five previous husbands and the man she was now living with wasn't her husband—and he told her that. Recognizing his prophetic skills, she switched the subject. "Sir," the woman said, "you must be a prophet. So tell me, why is it that you Jews insist that Jerusalem is the only place of worship, while we Samaritans claim it is here at Mount Gerizim, where our ancestors worshiped?" (verses 19–20). There's nothing better than a religious argument to divert attention from one's sordid past.

Something must have begun to dawn on her. This man was truly different. He had spoken to a strange woman, which was unusual. He was a Jewish man who spoke to a Samaritan, which was even more unusual. He asked her for her help and then offered to direct her to some unknown freshwater source. That was truly extraordinary. On top of all of that, he knew more about her than a lot of her friends did—the few she had left. This led her to inquire about spiritual things like worship and the Messiah.

So she stated her own belief: "I know the Messiah is coming—the one who is called Christ. When he comes, he will explain everything to us." Then Jesus revealed the truth of his relationship to her: "I AM the Messiah!" (verses 25–26). He was saying, "Yes, I may be a man, and I may be a Jewish man, but I'm really your Messiah, your deliverer, the one you have been longing for." At that point, her excitement was so great that she headed back to the village to spread the news of whom she had met.

This Samaritan woman had never encountered such a man—one who was so receptive, so open to her, so welcoming. She knew Jesus had no cause to love her the way he did. Being an immoral woman, she was rejected by most. She must have felt alienated and alone. But despite all that, this extraordinary Jesus received her with open arms.

His loving treatment of her didn't mean he approved of her adultery; he did not. Yet he didn't express disappointment toward her either. He still saw the beauty, the potential, and the innate worth and dignity God infused into every human by virtue of creation, and he loved her for it. Nor did he condemn her because she wasn't worshipping correctly. He loved her enough to tell her the truth. Jesus' love of her had nothing to do with her own actions. Nothing she could say or do or not say or not do would prevent Jesus from accepting her as he did, to show her such respect, and to let her know she was so welcome in his presence. He loved her as she was and gave her a vision of who she could be. That is the nature of Christlike love that welcomes another with open arms without necessarily approving of what he or she does or doesn't do.

Granted, loving others without approving of their behavior isn't always easy. Take a father like Todd. His son criticized him for being judgmental. Todd needs to guard his words and be careful when he talks about gay people. That includes never treating a person contrary to human dignity just because he or she is living contrary to God's commands. Otherwise, we'd soon be insulting everyone! After all, the Bible makes it clear that all have sinned and have lived contrary to God's commands (Romans 3:23; 1 John 1:10). Yet no matter how accepting we are, verbalizing disagreement with homosexuality often comes across as being judgmental.

I (Josh) know two women in their sixties who have lived together for decades. They claim they deeply love each other and that life together brings them meaning and happiness. How do I communicate that such a union is wrong without coming across as judgmental and intolerant? What is my responsibility to them? After all, Paul said we are not to judge outsiders (1 Corinthians 5:12–13). Does an accepting love sugarcoat the plain truth about God's design for marriage? If I'm too accepting and don't point out the wrong in such behavior, won't they feel that I am condoning their sexual choice? How can we stand up for biblical truth and avoid the judgmental label? Or can we?

It doesn't appear the Samaritan woman felt judged even though

Jesus didn't approve of her adultery. Most people Jesus encountered didn't feel judged by him, yet all of them were sinners in need of forgiveness. On the other hand, there were some whom Jesus did judge, like the hypocritical Pharisees that he referred to as "whitewashed tombs" (Matthew 23:27). They indeed felt judged. But after all, he was and is the final and righteous Judge. Can we hope to tell the truth to others and not be judgmental?

We believe it is not only possible, but scripture also gives us clear instructions on how we can accept people within the context of authentic love, which means judging their wrong behavior while at the same time not being judgmental. But as we have demonstrated through the illustrations of Chad and Todd and Renee and her parents, it is not always easy to stand for truth lovingly without compromising conviction. How do we take a stand for truth in a loving way? What does that sound like and look like? While the scripture gives us instructions on how to point out wrong, it also says, "Do not judge, or you too will be judged" (Matthew 7:1 NIV). Accepting without endorsing certain behaviors and speaking the truth while not judging—how do we do that? Let's journey on together to find out.

CHAPTER 7

KNOW THE TRUTH AND SPEAK IT IN LOVE

"Homosexuality is sinful," Todd stated emphatically to his son. "It's not the way God designed us—it's unnatural."

"Can you hear yourself, Dad?" Chad countered, shaking his head in disapproval. "You have no right to judge like that. You've got to accept people for who they are."

Is Chad right? When his dad claims that homosexuality is a sin against God's design, is he passing unwarranted judgment? Does he have a right to make such a judgment? How about Renee's father? He stated that it was flat wrong for her to sleep with her boyfriend. As Christians, can we be so definitive or dogmatic as to claim other people are wrong for what they do or say or believe to be true about themselves?

First, what Renee and Chad were reacting against most was the way their fathers were coming across to them. Renee felt that her dad was disappointed in her as a person. He made it quite clear she was violating what she was taught. Chad felt that his dad was attacking his friend's brother and rejecting him for who he was. There weren't a lot of warm and fuzzy feelings in the room with either family. Reactions and accusations normally escalate into emotional hurts when parents become emphatic and aggressive in expressing their beliefs. Such interactions rarely end well.

What we as parents want is to help our young people see why certain things are wrong and for them to make right choices in life. Yet in sharing the truth with our young people, especially on the bigger and highly controversial issues like sexual behavior, it's easy to focus more on the dos and don'ts and fail to consider the feelings involved. More often than not, emphasizing the rules tends to deemphasize the relationship. Whenever we share the truth with our young people, or with anyone else, for that matter, it is more effective when expressed in the context of a loving relationship that has the other's best interest at heart.

The apostle Paul wrote that we are to "speak the truth in love, growing in every way more and more like Christ" (Ephesians 4:15). Moral truth was meant to be experienced in the context of a loving relationship. All of God's truth comes from his loving, holy character and is meant to provide for us and protect us. He wants us to know that following his truth is always in our best interest (Deuteronomy 10:13).

The very reason we should want our young people, or anyone we know, to follow the instructions God has given us is because that is what is best for them. That is what love is about—it looks out for the best interest of another person. But does our love give us the right to make judgments about another's beliefs and behavior? Caring deeply for someone seems to be on the opposite end of the spectrum from judging his or her behavior.

TO JUDGE OR NOT TO JUDGE

What does scripture say?

> *"Judge not, that you be not judged."*
> (Matthew 7:1 NKJV)

If cultural tolerance had a theme verse, Matthew 7:1 would be it—a direct command, from Jesus no less, that we are not to judge others. This verse is one of the few remaining scriptures generally known in today's climate of declining biblical literacy, and the cultural thinking about it goes something like this: "Sure, scripture speaks against certain attitudes and actions and offers moral suggestions, but each of us is to interpret and apply those as we see fit. No one has the right to judge our actions as morally wrong. Jesus himself said so."

This verse is one of the most commonly misused in the Bible. The above interpretation takes it completely out of context. However, when we keep this one statement of Jesus within the entire context of his sermon, which begins in chapter 5, we capture the real meaning of his injunction, "Do not judge others."

Chapter 7 of Matthew is the continuation of Jesus' famous Sermon on the Mount. He begins his sermon with a statement about those who will enter the kingdom of God (Matthew 5:3). With this sermon Jesus is ushering into the world his new eternal kingdom. Throughout the sermon he continually calls people into that kingdom. So any interpretation of what he said within his sermon needs to be set within this context. Jesus is presenting an ethic for his disciples to follow. He is sharing the worldview they must follow if they are to be members of his eternal kingdom—how they are to think, be, and live within it.

When we understand this context, we can see clearly why Jesus tells us not to judge. His new kingdom already has a judge—a Righteous Judge who judges by the perfect standard of truth, which is God himself. God said, "It is mine to avenge; I will repay" (Deuteronomy 32:35 NIV). He told Israel to "not seek revenge or bear a grudge" (Leviticus 19:18). Why? Because judgment belongs to the Righteous Judge. When a person condemns another, he or she in effect presumes to determine who can and cannot be forgiven by God. This usurps God's rightful position as Judge.

Remember what Kenton said to his daughter? "I expect you to honor the morals and values your mother and I taught you all your life." Later he asked his wife, "Is she going to continue to go against what we have taught her and live an immoral life?" Whose standards of morality was this father most concerned with—his or God's? Sure, Kenton adopted biblical moral values as his own. But if he was personally offended because his daughter's behavior embarrassed or affronted him, Renee would have quickly picked up on that and sensed her dad's rejection. She naturally would not feel accepted.

Renee's real offense was first and foremost against the righteous King and Judge, Jesus himself. It was his instructions she was failing to follow. He had her best interest at heart when he created marriage as the context in which to experience sex. Was Jesus offended? Yes, but he did not write Renee off as a loss. She, like a lost sheep in his parable, had strayed from the safety of the kingdom, but she was worth rescuing—just as was the Samaritan woman, a greedy tax collector, or any other sinner he met. That's why Jesus was called a "friend of. . .sinners" (Luke 7:34).

But this didn't mean that Jesus abandoned his requirement that we follow what is moral and right. We must remember, however, that he is our model for how to present that standard. Every moral command from Jesus and the Bible comes from a heart of loving relationship with a desire to protect those he loves and provide for their best. If Kenton had captured the heart of Jesus, his attitude and words would have expressed compassion, care, and caution—all of which are in his daughter's emotional, relational, and spiritual best interest.

So does Matthew 7:1 tell us that since we live in the kingdom of the perfect judge, we are not to judge at all? No. The very next verse tells us that, "The standard you use *in judging* is the standard by which you will be judged" (Matthew 7:2, emphasis added). This makes it clear that we are to make judgments, but when we do, we must be careful to follow two rules: we must use the correct standard, and we must not presume to pass the sentence of condemnation.

Kenton's mistake was failing to use the current standard. He should have made it clear to Renee that it was not his personal standard she was violating; it was Jesus' standard. It is Jesus' character and nature that set the standard of morality, and from that standard God judges. When we lift up God's standard and make his relational heart known (rules in the context of relationships), we reflect godly judgment.

Many of the religious leaders of Jesus' day violated both the first and the second rules of judgment. They judged by the wrong standard, and they were a condemning group. They set themselves up in judgment of others using their own legalistic rules as the standard, and they did it with no concern for relationship, condemning without mercy anyone who violated their rules. Jesus didn't pull any punches when he addressed those who were so quick to see and judge the sins of others: "How can you think of saying to your friend, 'Let me help you get rid of that speck in your eye,' when you can't see past the log in your own eye? Hypocrite! First get rid of the log in your own eye; then you will see well enough to deal with the speck in your friend's eye" (Matthew 7:4–5).

Jesus was not telling his disciples never to make moral judgments. In fact, shortly thereafter he told them to beware of false prophets (7:15). Their first responsibility was to purify themselves by God's universal standard and then to make judgments concerning the behavior of others using the same standard. When God first gave his instructions to Israel he said, "Do not nurse hatred in your heart. . . . Confront people directly so you will not be held guilty for their sin" (Leviticus 19:17). This suggests that it is not wrong to address a wrong being done; rather, it is wrong to render judgment while harboring ill will toward the offender and hypocritically overlooking sin in our own lives. When we are aware of the sin in our own lives, we will be much more likely to show grace to others (Matthew 18:21–35).

When we look to God as the standard of right, not ourselves, we can judge rightly and truly see evil for what it is. The beauty of intolerance is its opposition to wrong and evil in the world—in alignment with God's righteous and perfect standard of justice, equality, human rights, and caring for others. Intolerance of evil is not mean-spirited and condemnatory; it is actually the only way to be loving and caring. Far from being judgmental, it advances God's righteous kingdom.

HUMBLY SPEAK THE TRUTH

When we speak the truth, even in love, we need to do so in humility. None of us has a corner on moral truth, which resides in and comes from God. When we stand up for a moral standard, we need to remember we are reflecting Christ and his standard.

One of the accusations that proponents of cultural tolerance make against Christians is that they are not only intolerant, but they are equally arrogant. Indeed, you may come across as arrogant if you claim to hold to a moral truth that applies to everyone, especially when that truth speaks directly to another person's sex life.

Of course people can be arrogant and right, or they can be arrogant and wrong. Conversely, people can equally be humble and right just as they can be humble and wrong. The attitude one has about truth is irrelevant to whether that truth is valid. Calling someone arrogant is an attack on the person—known as an *ad hominem*—and ignores the relevant question of truth. Christians should avoid personal attacks. Winning the argument about right or wrong isn't really the point. We can win the argument but lose the person. As Christians, we are to be "salt" and "light" to the world, letting our "good deeds shine out for all to see, so that everyone will praise [our] heavenly Father" (Matthew 5:16). When we are wise and faithful witnesses of God and his truth, he is honored.

Being wise about how we take a stand for truth isn't really that difficult. The key is to claim that the truth you are defending is not "your" truth. It comes from a source above you to which you are as responsible as everyone else.

A few years ago, I (Sean) was having a conversation with a nonbeliever about Christianity. He interrupted me and asked what right I had to claim that Jesus is the only way to salvation. "Isn't that being quite arrogant?" he asked. I simply replied, "I'm not being arrogant. Jesus is the one who makes the claim. Take it up with him."

I wasn't trying to be abrasive. I wanted to startle my friend into the realization that the sinless, virgin-born, miracle-working Savior is the one who claims to be the only way to God. I was in no position to make claims about the means of salvation; that was exclusively up to Jesus. You can defuse a possible argument and keep from falling into the trap of making others think you are claiming that "you own the corner on truth" by indicating that the morality you hold didn't originate with you. Explain that you have simply chosen to agree with the moral truths that Jesus proclaimed and the Bible propagates.

These universal moral truths are from God, and he has given them to us for our benefit. This is where we have an opportunity to share how God gave us moral truth for our own protection and well-being. Its purpose is not to keep us from enjoying life; it enables us to maximize life. Making it clear that the morality you believe in is biblical minimizes the accusation that you have set yourself up in judgment of others. Some may challenge your interpretation of the Bible and your understanding of the teachings of Jesus, so it is critical to have a ready defense for your views.

While it is important to humbly point people back to God and his Word as the ultimate authority on moral truth, there is no guarantee that others will respond positively. Jesus, the most humble of all, encountered accusations of arrogance. When he made himself known for who he really is, the religious leaders accused him of blasphemy. They said, "You, a mere man, claim to be God" (John 10:33).

Jesus went on to say, "If the world hates you, remember that it hated me first. The world would love you as one of its own if you belonged to it, but you are no longer part of the world" (John 15:18–19). No matter how lovingly and humbly we speak the truth, some will still reject God's message and possibly hate us for it. To paraphrase what my (Sean's) mentor Greg Koukl often says, "We shouldn't add any offense to the gospel, but we certainly shouldn't take any away. It's already offensive enough! If people hate us, just be sure it's for genuinely following the teachings of Jesus rather than for an unbiblical attitude."

KNOW THE TRUTH

Another thing some Christians fail to do is interpret God's truth accurately. You have probably heard people claim the 9/11 attacks were God's judgment on a sinful nation. Others have said that AIDS is a result of God's anger toward gays. Practically every time a natural disaster strikes, someone claims it is God's judgment on the wickedness in the world. To avoid casting a bad light on a righteous but merciful God, we should do our homework before we speak and not make assumptions we cannot justify.

Looking again at sexual morality, does God's Word really say and mean that premarital sex and homosexual acts are sinful? If so, why? Some people see homosexual acts as wrong because they find them disgusting. Others think teenage premarital sex is wrong because teens are too immature to engage in sex. But these are not the reasons God established boundaries on sex.

As we have already mentioned, scripture is clear when it commands: "Let there be no sexual immorality, impurity, or greed among you" (Ephesians 5:3). When we engage in sexual immorality, whether it is extramarital or premarital sex, pornography, or incest, it is wrong because it is outside the boundaries of God's intended expression—marriage. Purity before marriage (Hebrews 13:4) and fidelity within marriage (Exodus 20:14) are the loving boundaries God has set in which sexual activity is to take place.

When the apostle Paul wrote his letter to the church in Corinth, it was not unlike our culture today. The reputation of the city of Corinth was that it was full of vice and all manner of sexual sins. The church community he wrote to was multiethnic and was being influenced by a corrupt culture. He contrasted the so-called sexual freedom of the Greco-Roman culture with the sexual life of God's people within the boundaries of a loving marriage of faithfulness and purity between a man and a woman. Paul, writing under the guidance and inspiration of God, made it clear that sex with anyone outside of a relationship between a married man and woman was wrong. Here is what Paul wrote:

> *Don't you realize that those who do wrong will not inherit the Kingdom of God? Don't fool yourselves. Those who indulge in sexual sin, or who worship idols, or commit adultery, or are male prostitutes, or practice homosexuality, or are thieves, or greedy people, or drunkards, or are abusive, or cheat people—*

none of these will inherit the Kingdom of God. . . .

You can't say that our bodies were made for sexual immorality. They were made for the Lord, and the Lord cares about our bodies. . . .

Run from sexual sin! No other sin so clearly affects the body as this one does. For sexual immorality is a sin against your own body. . . . So you must honor God with your body. . . .

Because there is so much immorality, each man should have his own wife, and each woman should have her own husband.

The husband should fulfill his wife's sexual needs, and the wife should fulfill her husband's needs. The wife gives authority over her body to her husband, and the husband gives authority over his body to his wife. (1 Corinthians 6:9–10, 13, 18–20; 7:2–4)

Here Paul tells us unambiguously what sexual immorality is—premarital sex, prostitution, pornography, homosexual acts, and adultery—and that it is wrong. Why is sexual immorality wrong? In the passages above, Paul himself gives us a primary reason: our bodies were not made for immorality. When a person commits acts of sexual immorality, he or she is doing something the body was never designed to do. As sexual beings, a man and a woman are designed to experience a sexual union within the confines of marriage—the two are made to enjoy each other sexually. A man is meant to give himself fully to his wife, and the woman is meant to give herself fully to her husband. This unselfish devotion to one another is the formula for emotional, relational, and sexual intimacy.

When we engage in sexual acts outside of marriage, we violate God's loving boundaries and do wrong against ourselves. God never intended sexual behavior to take place other than within the loving bonds of marriage.

Some religious teachers asked Jesus if a man could divorce his wife for any reason. Jesus referred back to the reality that God originally made marriage between a man and a woman as a permanent union. In referencing Genesis chapters 1 and 2, Jesus reminded them of scriptures recording "that from the beginning 'God made male and female.'" And he said, "This explains why a man leaves his father and mother and is joined to his wife, and the two are united into one" (Matthew 19:4–5).

From the beginning God defined marriage between a man and a woman as a permanent union of the heart and the body. The man is drawn away from his family of origin and makes a commitment to love a woman. And when they unite in one heart and one body sexually, they form a marriage union and become "one flesh." According to Jesus, sex was meant to be experienced within the exclusive, permanent union of one man and one woman in God's lovingly designed institution of marriage.

In effect, God is telling us that to engage in sex outside of marriage is not what he originally intended. He wants what is best for our sex life. Those who advocate same-sex marriage claim it is not unnatural or a distortion—it is simply extending the marriage institution to same-sex couples. Paul ties sexual immorality to idolatry (Colossians 3:5). To go against God's design for marriage is to rebel against our Creator (and his design for us) and declare ourselves our own gods. In a sermon on Romans 1, John Piper observed:

> *The reason Paul focuses on homosexuality in these verses is because it is the most vivid dramatization in life of the profoundest connection between the disordering of heart-worship and the disordering of our sexual lives. I'll try to say it*

simply, though it is weighty beyond words.

We learn from Paul in Ephesians 5:31–32 that, from the beginning, manhood and womanhood existed to represent or dramatize God's relation to his people and then Christ's relation to his bride, the church. In this drama, the man represents God or Christ and is to love his wife as Christ loved the church. The woman represents God's people or the church. And sexual union in the covenant of marriage represents pure, undefiled, intense heart-worship. That is, God means for the beauty of worship to be dramatized in the right ordering of our sexual lives.

But instead, we have exchanged the glory of God for images, especially of ourselves. The beauty of heart-worship has been destroyed. Therefore, in judgment, God decrees that this disordering of our relation to him be dramatized in the disordering of our sexual relations with each other. And since the right ordering of our relationship to God in heart-worship was dramatized by heterosexual union in the covenant of marriage, the disordering of our relationship to God is dramatized by the breakdown of that heterosexual union.

Homosexuality is the most vivid form of that breakdown. God and man in covenant worship are represented by male and female in covenant sexual union. Therefore, when man turns from God to images of himself, God hands us over to what we have chosen and dramatizes it by male and female turning to images of themselves for sexual union, namely their own sex. Homosexuality is the judgment of God dramatizing the exchange of the glory of God for images of ourselves. (See the parallel uses of "exchange" in verses 25 and 26.)[1]

The problem with the revisionist view of marriage is that the nature of marriage is not something that an individual or a community or a society decides, any more than it can "decide" the nature of gravity. A society can decide to call a different relationship "marriage," or decide to give marriage licenses to same-sex couples, but that doesn't change the objective nature of marriage itself. According to scripture, God has already decided it. John Stonestreet, executive director of the Chuck Colson Center for Christian Worldview, and I (Sean) coauthored a book about same-sex marriage. In the book, we list three essential characteristics of biblical marriage:

> *First,* marriage is two human beings becoming one in every way possible. . . . *In marriage, two become one, united in mind and body and purpose.*
>
> *Second,* marriage is oriented toward procreation. *The act of two becoming one flesh makes God's intent, that humans should "fill" and "form" his world, possible. . . . Scripture sees marriage as being closely tied to procreation. . . .*
>
> *Third,* marriage comes with an expectation of permanence. *The Genesis account implies marriage is a permanent relationship, [but] Jesus' words are explicit: "What therefore God has joined together, let not man separate" (Matthew 19:6). . . .*

> *Therefore we shouldn't think of marriage as a political institution that belongs to the state. It is a pre-political institution. The state doesn't create marriage; it can only recognize it. The state, despite all its efforts, will never be able to redefine marriage. Marriage will always be what marriage was created to be, no matter what activist judges, runaway legislatures or majority of voters decide.[2]*

Sex and marriage between a man and a woman are intrinsically linked together by God's design. That is where the discussion needs to center with your family. What your children hear about the "gay versus Christian" morality debate is often centered on how Christians allegedly discriminate against same-sex marriages and wrongfully label the gay community as sinful. We need to help them refocus the argument. It needs to shift away from who is accusing whom of judging or whether it's right to legislate morality. We must focus our young peoples' discussion on who has the right to define morality in the first place. We need to help them see that only God is in the position to say what moral behavior honors him and is in our own best interest. He is the true righteous Judge.

Questions about homosexual behavior, same-sex marriage, and even premarital sex are to be decided not by us, but by God himself. Understanding and properly interpreting what the Bible says about sexual morality will give you a God-focused framework for interacting with others. When you are armed with knowledge of the scriptural truth, you are prepared to guide others to what God has to say on the subject and how he always has our best interest at heart.

EXAMPLES OF KNOWING AND SPEAKING THE TRUTH IN LOVE

Now, imagine the difference it could make if Renee's parents, Kenton and Teri, had equipped their minds with scriptural knowledge and their hearts with the love and humility of Christ when they interacted with their daughter. What if Todd had done the same thing with his son? Let's replay the interactions of both of these families and see how things go when these parents are better equipped in both mind and heart.

"My Pancake Special"

"You'll love him, Mom," Renee gushed on her visit home from her second year in college. "He's so considerate, he's smart, and he's really good looking."

Teri smiled. "That's great honey," she said. "What's he majoring in?"

"Business management, just like me."

"That's good. Does he have your same church background, too?"

"Mom," Renee responded with a tinge of irritation. "Let's not get into church stuff again."

"I'm not," Teri replied. "I just wanted to know if he shares our family's values, that's all."

"Tony doesn't go to church, okay? He's not an atheist or anything; he's just not into church and religious stuff."

"Who's not into religious stuff?" The voice was that of Renee's father, Kenton, who had just walked into the room.

"Renee was just telling me about her new friend, Tony," Teri replied. "She said he isn't into church."

"What is he, an atheist?" Kenton asked.

"Come on, you guys," Renee retorted. "Tony's a great guy! Whether he goes to church or not isn't an issue with me."

"I see," Kenton responded. "When do we get to meet this great guy anyway?"

"Actually, we were hoping we could both come here for Christmas break—not for the entire two weeks, of course. We want to spend part of it with his parents, too. But at least long enough that you can get to know each other."

"That's a wonderful idea, honey," Teri said. "Your dad and I would love it. Just let us know ahead of time which days you'll be here, and I'll have the guest room ready."

Renee hesitated. "Sure Mom, but—" She took a deep breath. "Well, like, is the guest room really necessary? I was thinking we could just stay in my room together."

"Oh," Kenton responded with a sigh. Teri sat silently trying to keep her face from showing the disappointment she felt inside.

"I know it's a lot to ask and everything," Renee began. "But since Tony and I are rooming together at college anyway, I thought we could room together here, too."

Teri's heart pounded like drums. She looked over at Kenton, his shoulders slumped—his eyes gazing at the floor. Teri spoke first.

"You must really like Tony."

"I do, Mom. In fact, we're in love."

"Love's a great thing," Teri replied. "Your dad and I fell in love while we were in college. But we didn't sleep together before we were married. We weren't perfect, but we avoided a lot of the pain we saw our friends go through because they didn't wait."

"I hear you," Renee responded. "But that's a bit old-fashioned these days."

"It probably does seem old-fashioned," Kenton chimed in, speaking softly. "But the emotional, spiritual, and possible physical consequences aren't old-fashioned at all."

"I know all about safe sex, Dad," Renee responded quickly.

"It's more than about safe sex, honey. What your mom and I are trying to say is that you mean the world to us, and we want what's best for you—so does God. This is from my heart: You'll never regret waiting, but. . ." Kenton's voice cracked. He paused to regain his composure. "But you may always regret not waiting."

Teri stepped toward her daughter, her eyes blurred with tears, and wrapped her arms around her.

"I love you, honey."

"I love you, too, Mom," Renee whispered. As the two drew apart, a small tear could be seen in the corner of Renee's eye. She took a deep breath.

"I know you guys love me. That means a lot. So about Tony—when he's here we'll sleep in separate rooms. And I promise I will think about what you guys have said."

Kenton stood and took a deep breath.

"Hey," he said, smiling. "How about ol' Dad fixing my pancake special for my college girl?"

"That sounds fantastic, Dad."

Kenton and Teri may not have changed Renee's moral values, and she may still continue sleeping with her boyfriend. But because they shared God's moral truth within the context of their loving hearts, Renee heard them out. The relationship with their daughter is intact, maybe stronger than ever. And future opportunities are left open for them to continue to have a positive influence in the life of their daughter as she continues to make her moral choices. God is powerfully at work as his truth is spoken in love.

"May I Join You?"

"We're out of here," seventeen-year-old Chad called out to his dad as he and his friend Mike headed toward the door.

"Where you going so fast?" asked Chad's father, Todd.

"The GG9 is having its track and field this afternoon," Chad replied. "So Mike and I are going to watch."

"The GG what?" Todd inquired.

"Dad, it's been all over the news. Aren't you up on it?"

"Up on what? I don't know what you're talking about."

"Mr. Arnold," Mike responded, "the GG9 is the international Gay Games, something like the Olympics, that happens every four years. And this year part of it is in our city. My older brother is running in the relay race today."

"Ohhhhh, those games. Yeah, I've read about some about them. What event are you interested in?"

"My brother's race starts in about an hour," Mike said.

I'm not wild about my son going to these games, Todd thought. *But maybe there's an opportunity here.*

"Would you guys mind if I join you? I used to run the relay myself."

Chad and Mike looked at each other and shrugged in unison.

"Sure, Dad, come on. There's no entrance fee or anything." Chad waved his arm toward the door.

As Todd drove the two boys to the games, he learned that Mike's brother had recently told his parents, who were divorced, that he was gay. Todd asked how his parents handled that news. Mike replied that it was not well received. His dad told his brother he couldn't stay at his house, and his dad hadn't spoken to his brother since.

After the relay race was over, Todd dropped Mike off at his house. On the drive home Todd posed a question to his son.

"What do you think about how Mike's dad responded to his brother being gay?"

"I think it really sucks," Chad stated bluntly.

"Yeah, it's gotta really hurt Mike, too. But why do you think his dad won't even talk to his brother?" Todd probed.

"His dad probably hates gays, and now that his son's gay, he probably hates him, too."

"You know something, son? You don't have to hate someone

just because you disapprove of what he does."

Chad was listening intently. Todd went on.

"I did a lot of wrong things when I was younger, and God disapproved of every one of them. But he still loved and accepted me for who I was. God is our model for how we can disagree with what a person does and still accept them for the person God created them to be."

Chad absorbed every word that came out of Todd's mouth.

"And you know, son, accepting a person for who they are without approving of their behavior is the kind of friendship I think Mike and his brother need."

Todd went on to share how he and his son could befriend Mike's brother. Because Todd was willing to walk through a "Samaria," a place where most Christians won't go, he was able to demonstrate godly acceptance before his son. Chad knew his dad didn't believe homosexual behavior was right. But by being accepting enough to watch a relay run by gay participants, Todd is in a great position to mold the mind and heart of his son in the right direction.

These two stories ended well. We don't mean to imply that this always happens. In fact, many times it doesn't. Having a loving heart toward young people, and being willing to speak truth in love, often requires patience and a long-suffering heart. There simply is no "magic bullet" for getting children (especially *adult* children) to do the right thing. As painful as it is, sometimes love requires that parents stand by and watch children do the wrong thing. Having a long-term perspective can help alleviate the pressure to feel like you have to "fix" young people in the present moment. Remember, God loves them more than we do, and his heart aches even more deeply to see them return to him (cf. Luke 13:34).

Not long ago I (Sean) attended The Reformation Project conference, which is part of a larger movement committed to reforming the church's traditional views on homosexuality.[3] My goal was simply to meet people and learn about the movement from the inside. Along with worship, testimonies, and lectures, there were multiple ninety-minute sessions focused on helping people rebut biblical arguments against homosexuality and to make the most compelling case for the compatibility of Christianity and same-sex relationships. These sessions were led by authors Matthew Vines (*God and the Gay Christian*) and James Brownson (*Bible, Gender, Sexuality*).

Afterward the leaders broke us up into small groups and sent us to classrooms to practice what we had learned by role-playing. As the group session started, the teacher went to the front of the class and said, "Before we begin the role play, it would be great if everyone could share your story of why you are here and why you care so much about this movement." Inside I was thinking: *You've got to be kidding me. How did I get myself into this situation? What should I say?* Fortunately, I was fifteenth out of twenty people, so I had some time to think and pray for wisdom.

Even though I had serious theological reservations with the views of others in the group, I was heartbroken at many of their stories. One young man shared how his church kicked him out when they found that he was gay. A young woman shared how her parents rejected her when she came out as a lesbian. An older man shared how he had experienced same-sex attraction his entire life, and because of his shame, he had never told anyone until last week. He first told his mother, who was sixty years old. My heart broke for many of these people.

It was finally my turn. I started with, "My name is Sean McDowell, and I teach at Biola University." Many of them must have known about Biola and its conservative biblical stance, because half of them looked at me with an expression of surprise and bewilderment, as if they were wondering, *Who let this guy in here?* I continued, "If you are familiar with Biola, then you probably realize I am not theologically where you want me to be. In fact, I have serious theological reservations about what I am hearing here. But I want to read you something."

I pulled out the worship packet we were given at registration and read them the opening words, "There is love for one like you. There is grace enough to see you through. And wherever you have walked, whatever path you choose, may you know there is love for one like you." I then turned and asked, "We may disagree theologically, but there's a place for me here, right?" At that point, they had to say yes, or they would have betrayed their message of inclusion and tolerance. And many of them graciously welcomed me.

I went on, "Like you, I am here because the church desperately needs to get this answer right. I have seen the pain firsthand that many of my students and friends with same-sex attraction have experienced. I am here to meet many of you, to learn about your views firsthand, and to understand where you are coming from so maybe I can gain some insight about how to best address this issue."

I paused and then made my final point. "The narrative often told is that those who don't affirm homosexuality are hateful, bigoted, homophobic, and intolerant. I want you to know that this is not always true. There are Christians who have serious reservations about your theology but still love you as people. I am not homophobic, or I wouldn't be here. There are many Christians who care deeply about each one of you. And I am sorry many of you have experienced such hurt at the hands of believers. But please don't be tempted to think we hate you just because we disagree with your views."

Unfortunately, I had to leave soon afterward to catch a flight. But I have been in touch with a handful of people in that classroom since, and from what I can tell, they were touched by my comments.

Be a student of God's Word. Know why you believe sexual immorality is wrong—know the positive provision and protection that comes by following God's instructions on morality. And then seek to speak the truth in love. Capture God's heart, knowing that he wants only what is best for us. Share how your own obedience to God's Word has brought you protection and provision. Let your children know you love them. Accept them for who they are as your children regardless of what they have done. As you keep at it, you will increase your opportunities to instill godly values deep within their hearts.

> *The LORD is good and does what is right; he shows the proper path to those who go astray. He leads the humble in doing right, teaching them his way. The LORD leads with unfailing love and faithfulness all who keep his covenant and obey his demands. (Psalm 25:8–10)*

> *Repeat [God's commands] again and again to your children. Talk about them when you are at home and when you are on the road, when you are going to bed and when you are getting up. (Deuteronomy 6:7)*

CHAPTER 8

CULTURAL TOLERANCE AND EDUCATION

Emily stood at the front door, packed and ready to leave for a high school–sponsored weekend with her friend Terilyn.

"When do you get home from this conference thing with Terilyn?" her mother asked, fluffing her daughter's hair as she spoke.

"It's a three-day conference," Emily replied. "We'll be back Sunday evening about six."

"And what is this conference, exactly?"

Emily had told her mother about the conference before, but not *exactly*. If she had told everything, her mother would have freaked out and slammed the door on the whole weekend.

"It's the Young Women's Leadership Conference at the Hilton in San Francisco," she said. "Terilyn says it's the best way to get into the student government at Hoover High School. The student council adviser is taking ten girls from Hoover, and Terilyn got me in."

It was all true. But what Emily was *not* telling her mother was that the conference included a major unit on tolerance.

After checking into the downtown Hilton the next day, Emily and Terilyn went for pizza with Hoover's student adviser, Lisa Carmona. They were discussing the topics of the conference listed in the program, when one of the other students said that she sometimes got confused when people talked about tolerance. She wasn't sure what it really meant, sometimes.

"Tolerance is the highest of all virtues," Ms. Carmona said, smiling. "It is the highest virtue because it acknowledges and celebrates the personal rights and values of all cultures and peoples. But it is often misunderstood because some people in our culture have improperly defined it."

Ms. Carmona twirled her soda straw between her manicured fingers. "The virtue of tolerance is based on the reality that everyone is equal in value. Nobody at this table is better than anyone else, right?" The girls nodded as if on cue. "That's right. We're different from each other in a lot of ways, but we're all equal in value. And if all cultures and all persons are equal in value, then all lifestyles are equal, too. Tolerance is simply accepting and celebrating another person's beliefs and lifestyle choices."

Emily nodded along with the other girls. She wondered if her mom and dad would find something wrong with Ms. Carmona's ideas, but Emily sure couldn't find any fault with them herself. After all, Ms. Carmona was a teacher; she obviously knew what she was talking about.

The above story, while fictional, is based on actual events happening today in community after community. As you read Ms. Carmona's description of tolerance, it actually sounds quite good until she uses her accurate premise, "If all cultures and all persons are equal in value. . ." to reach a false conclusion: ". . .then all lifestyles are equal, too." That is not only an unwarranted assumption; it is an incorrect one. All persons are of equal value before God, but all choices and lifestyles definitely are not. And the problem is that this one clause—"then all lifestyles are equal, too"—in Ms. Carmona's definition is at the core of the culture's push for tolerance.

A generation or more ago, schools focused primarily on such subjects as English, history, math, and science. Today one significant educational goal—at the primary, secondary, and college levels—is for students to learn a variety of subjects through the lens of cultural tolerance.

Short of complete isolation from society, how do we counter the influence of cultural tolerance our children are subjected to within the educational system? A growing number of Christian parents have elected to educate their children through homeschooling. Others have enrolled their children in Christian schools. Many, however, still rely on the public school system for their children's education. That being the case, what can we do to diminish the effects of cultural tolerance and the moral relativism it spawns? First and foremost, we must become thoroughly acquainted with what the doctrine of cultural tolerance teaches—understanding it is based in a cultural narrative about truth. We must also equip ourselves with the biblical narrative about truth that comes from the loving heart of God, and in a Christlike manner, speak his truth boldly yet in love. These past seven chapters have been devoted to providing guidance toward that goal.

When you are armed with a Christlike attitude and a biblically based message (more accurately a biblical worldview), God is able to empower and lead you to lovingly counter the culture. Countering cultural tolerance within education is largely a matter of awareness. Become aware of what is taking place in the hallways, classrooms, and educator-sponsored outings of your child's school. This requires open communications with your children about what is going on in school. It also requires taking the initiative to learn from teachers and administrators what is being taught and how it is being taught.

GET ACQUAINTED WITH YOUR SCHOOL'S CURRICULUM AND WHO IS TEACHING YOUR CHILD

Discover how your children are being educated at school. Get exposed to the classroom curriculum they are using and the mind-set, philosophy, and educational worldview of those who teach them.

The public school system employs teachers who have successfully attended universities and earned education degrees. The educational worldview engrained within most public and private universities, which inevitably influences teachers, is one of cultural tolerance and its moral relativism. Duke Pesta, professor at the University of Wisconsin–Oshkosh, makes this astute observation about the consequences of moral relativism on the educational system and those being trained to teach our children:

> *For thousands of years, the chief aim and civilizing purpose of education had been moral development, an incessant recognition of the limits of human wisdom in the face of the divine, and an insistent reminder of the greater, unseen moral order that underpins the naturalistic world of the jungle, a world where power alone dictates right, and mere survival at any cost equals "truth" in the rawest, most naked sense of the word. Yet the educational paradigms of today—manifested most acutely in the morally relativistic approaches of the humanities—actually reinforce this Darwinian primacy of nature, and work against civilization.*
>
> *It starts at the top, in the journal articles and published books that secure tenure and impose the ideological dictates determining the construction of curricula, the pedagogy taught in graduate programs, and the way we train teachers from kindergarten through high school and beyond. At the highest levels of academia, the tenured professoriate—and the professors, deans, provosts, chancellors, and university presidents who almost always arise from the privileged ranks of this tenured class—there exists a dangerously monolithic echo chamber, where relativistic, post-modern ideas about*

the world, culture, and truth have become calcified. The consequences to education of this ideological conformity can be witnessed at every level of public, and in many cases private, instruction, for many private schools only hire teachers trained and certified by state-run education programs. The dominance of moral relativism in our humanities curricula, from kindergarten through graduate school, guarantees that the study of philosophy, history, art, and literature amounts to little more than an amoral, un-reflexive acknowledgment of the random, chaotic, arbitrary, and ultimately meaningless nature of "reality."[1]

Consequently, many teachers view all learning through the lens of moral relativism from the start. They see cultural tolerance as the moral glue that holds schools together. This perspective is reinforced by the curriculum that teachers are assigned to use in the classroom, and it often trumps the moral values that the church and Christian families are trying to instill within their children. This, in effect, signals to your child that what the school teaches on moral values should be embraced even if parents or churches teach otherwise.

Throughout the United States, Canada, and other Western nations, books and classes have been revised to make schools more "inclusive," more "diverse," more "sensitive," "gender neutral," "antiracist," and "disability aware." Some of these changes are positive, of course. It is good for students to learn not only about William Shakespeare and George Washington but also about Sequoyah (the inventor of the Cherokee alphabet), Martin Luther King Jr., and Gandhi. It is good for us all to learn from the often-neglected music, literature, drama, and customs of other cultures.

But some of the studies and curriculum in the public school

system go beyond that. They advocate a cultural narrative about truth that denies the existence of any moral truth outside of what a person chooses to believe. Some curriculum goes so far as to teach a child the difference between fact and opinion by reinforcing that all values and moral claims are a matter of opinion only.

Justin McBrayer is an associate professor of philosophy at Fort Lewis College in Durango, Colorado. To acquaint himself with how his second-grade son was being taught, he visited the classroom during open house. He said he found a troubling pair of signs hanging over the bulletin board. They read:

> *Fact: Something that is true about a subject and*
> *can be tested or proven.*
> *Opinion: What someone thinks, feels, or believes.*

Motivated by the words on the signs, professor McBrayer researched the curriculum to answer a troubling question: How does the dichotomy between fact and opinion relate to morality?

Here is what he discovered:

> *I learned the answer to this question only after I investigated*
> *my son's homework (and other examples of assignments online).*
> *Children are asked to sort facts from opinions and, without*
> *fail, every value claim is labeled as an opinion. Here's a little*
> *test devised from questions available on fact vs. opinion*
> *worksheets online:*
>
> > *Are the following facts or opinions?*
> > ___ Copying homework assignments is wrong.
> > ___ Cursing in school is inappropriate behavior.

___ All men are created equal.

___ It is worth sacrificing some personal liberties to protect our country from terrorism.

___ It is wrong for people under the age of 21 to drink alcohol.

___ Vegetarians are healthier than people who eat meat.

___ Drug dealers belong in prison.

The answer? In each case, the worksheets categorize these claims as opinions. The explanation was that each of these claims is a value claim, and value claims are not facts. This is repeated ad nauseum: any claim with good, right, wrong, etc. is not a fact.

In summary, our public schools teach students that all claims are either facts or opinions and that all value and moral claims fall into the latter camp. The punchline: there are no moral facts. And if there are no moral facts, then there are no moral truths.[2]

This isn't to say all public school teachers and administrators are sinister disciples of moral relativism intent on indoctrinating your children in cultural tolerance. Many of them are decent, upstanding citizens who care about children. Most teach because they love seeing students learn. Yet many well-meaning educators simply fail to see the danger or the damage that the doctrine of cultural tolerance has done and is doing. On the other hand, we must recognize that there are teachers who aggressively attempt to indoctrinate their students in cultural relativism and shame those who reject it.

USE CULTURAL TOLERANCE EXTREMISM TO YOUR ADVANTAGE

Because scripture admonishes us to speak the truth in love doesn't mean we are not to speak up against injustice and prejudice toward Christians who have the right to freedom of religion in America. Take advantage of instances that garner news headlines, especially those that attack common sense and your child's freedom of religion in the name of cultural tolerance. See them as opportunities to speak up and share with friends and educators how unreasonable cultural tolerance can be.

For example, consider the case of a twelve-year-old boy who was told he could not read the Bible during free reading time at school. A Florida teacher at Park Lake's Elementary School in Fort Lauderdale ordered young Giovanni Rubeo to pick up the phone on her desk and punch in the number of his parents.

As the other students watched, the teacher took the phone from Giovanni's hands and left a terse message on the family's answering machine. "I noticed that he has a book—a religious book—in the classroom," she said on the recording. "He's not permitted to read those books in my classroom."[3]

This was not a student pounding the table and waving his Bible over his head, declaring, "You are all going to hell unless you accept Jesus." This was a twelve-year-old boy quietly reading scripture to himself during free reading time. Obviously, the teacher went to extremes in an attempt at creating "greater diversity." It is amazing how voices that are diverse from the official lockstep thinking are excluded in the name of "diversity."

Use these kinds of instances to discuss the problem with fellow parents and even teachers. Point out how respecting others of different beliefs and faith doesn't warrant the shaming of those who respect and revere the Bible. Acquaint yourself with what religious activity is and is not permitted in a public school by the US Department of Education. The truth is, the DOE guidelines *do* allow students to read their Bibles during noninstructional time. The guidelines read in part: "Students may read their Bibles or other scriptures, say grace before meals, and pray or study religious materials with fellow students during recess, the lunch hour, or other noninstructional time to the same extent that they may engage in nonreligious activities."[4]

While extreme incidents like the one in Fort Lauderdale have been rare, they are becoming more and more prevalent, especially as Christians throughout America make their voices heard. Consider the following cases:

- A school employee tells a five-year-old student she can't pray over her lunch.[5]
- A teacher refuses to let a ten-year-old student write about God for a school assignment.[6]
- School officials tell students to stop praying to Jesus and singing "Amazing Grace" together during free time.[7]

Some of these actions by school officials seem hard to believe. It appears in those situations that religious freedom and common sense have been thrown out the window. It is clear there are those in the public educational system who are intent on enforcing diversity as defined by cultural tolerance, even if it means trampling on the freedom of religion. And yet it is important to realize that *most* educators and administrators don't have a hidden secular agenda—they primarily want to help children develop and learn. And yet there are certainly a few agenda-driven influential educators, like those, who act with ignorance and (possibly) malice toward believers.

Perhaps one of the more egregious and extreme examples of cultural tolerance in the classroom surfaced when Ryan Rotela refused to engage in a classroom exercise at Florida Atlantic University (FAU).

Communications instructor Dr. Deandre Poole asked students to write "Jesus" on a piece of paper then stomp on it.[8] The incident gained statewide attention when acting Governor Rick Scott got involved. He wrote FAU chancellor Frank Brogan, saying, "The professor's lesson was offensive, and even intolerant, to Christians and those of all faiths who deserve to be respected as Americans entitled to religious freedom."[9]

The university initially defended the classroom activity drawn from an instruction manual on intercultural communication. The exercise was designed to prompt discussion about the importance of symbols in culture. The university eventually apologized and said professors would not be using the exercise again.

RESPOND RATHER THAN REACT

Refraining from reacting aggressively to some of these extremes is difficult. It's not that these incidents shouldn't anger us; in fact, they should. Scripture, however, admonishes, "Don't sin by letting anger control you" (Ephesians 4:26). A loving and possibly firm response is better than an angry reaction.

Here are some suggestions as to how you might respond to a public educational system that is teaching in the context of cultural tolerance.

- There is effectiveness in numbers. Gather other

Christian parents who have children enrolled in your public school district. Establish a strategy to monitor what your schools are teaching. Pledge to work together as a coalition of parents who are committed to instilling biblical values in your children.

- Remember that *you*, not their teachers, not their principals, and not their school or school board, are in charge of your children's education. Pay attention to what they are being taught; browse through their textbooks; drop into an occasional assembly; chaperone a field trip now and then. Express any concerns in a gracious manner (Colossians 4:6), and make an extra effort to express appreciation when the school or teacher shows sensitivity to or support for your rights as a parent.

- Make every effort to build strong relationships with your children's teachers, principals, superintendents, school board members, PTA presidents, and school janitors. Attend open houses. Ask for teachers' e-mail addresses. Learn which teachers (and others) share your values and convictions and which do not—not so that you may "get rid of" the wrong-minded individuals but to better understand them and, when necessary, counter their influence and ideas.

- Look for opportunities to express kindness and appreciation toward teachers and administrators. Make it your goal to perform at least two loving acts for every criticism or concern you express to a school official.

- Don't shy away from confronting those who aggressively try to indoctrinate your children in an extreme application of cultural tolerance. "Be quick to listen, slow to speak, and slow to get angry" (James 1:19). Act wisely with a Christlike attitude, but do act. Enlist your parent coalition to act with you.

- Keep the lines of communication open with your children. Make it a practice to ask about their day, how it went in school, what was the most interesting thing that happened, what was the most boring, and so on. Let them know you are sincerely interested in them, what they are learning, and how their teachers are teaching them.

Remember above all the power of your own influence in the lives of your children. Be a role model who "speak[s] the truth in love, growing in every way more and more like Christ" (Ephesians 4:15). You have an advantage over public school educators. You have a loving relationship with your children that opens them up to receive from you much more than they will ever receive from someone else. Cherish that relationship; build it deep and strong. As you do, you will have a fighting chance to instill your values and a love for God in your children so that they can live as "'children of God without fault in a warped and crooked generation.' Then you will shine among them like the stars in the sky" (Philippians 2:15 NIV).

CHAPTER 9

CULTURAL TOLERANCE AND THE GOVERNMENT

Congress shall make no law respecting an establishment of religion, or prohibiting the free exercise thereof; or abridging the freedom of speech, or of the press; or the right of the people peaceably to assemble, and to petition the Government for a redress of grievances.

This First Amendment to the US Constitution was added to guarantee the religious civil liberties of the citizenry. It was designed to erect a "wall of separation," so to speak, between church and state, which meant that the state was not to infringe on the free expression of religion by American citizens.

For much of the past two centuries, Christians in America and other Western nations have generally enjoyed freedom of worship and expression of their faith in the public square. Christianity by its very nature is missional—that is, its influence is meant to go beyond the private and devotional exercise of a person worshipping God in his or her own home or church building. A follower of Christ is supposed to live out his or her faith in the world. This kind of active, outgoing faith has implications for society, including its morality and laws, as well as its educational, emotional, physical, spiritual, and relational well-being. Over the past few decades, however, some proponents of cultural tolerance have sought to limit that influence. This brings clearly into focus the fact that two conflicting views of truth are at odds with one another. Christians have a mission, as the apostle Paul stated: "God has given us this task of reconciling people to him" (2 Corinthians 5:18). That task is not welcome in a culture that contends there is no singular truth or one true God to which people are to be reconciled.

KINGDOMS IN CONFLICT

Jesus came to earth to offer salvation to the entire world. He did not claim simply to be the God of the Jewish nation. He is the Creator God of all that exists and the only means to rescue humans from the death sentence of sin. His kingdom had been contaminated by sin, so his mission included reestablishing his righteous kingdom (Matthew 4:23). After Jesus was crucified and rose again, his followers met with him many times. He talked with them often about the kingdom. Finally, they asked, "Lord, has the time come for you to free Israel and restore our kingdom?" (Acts 1:6). He replied that his Father set such dates as those, and it was not for them to know. Furthermore, he announced that he was about to leave them again. But he promised to send his Holy Spirit, who would empower them to spread his kingdom "in Jerusalem, throughout Judea, in Samaria, and to the ends of the earth" (Acts 1:8).

No doubt such answers confused these followers even more. Why wouldn't Jesus move to establish himself as the righteous ruler of his kingdom now? Why would he leave them in his moment of greatest triumph? And how could they establish his kingdom without its leader? Jesus was truly the leader of the kingdom movement, but his idea of the kingdom was considerably different from that of his disciples and the rest of the world. The religious leaders didn't understand it, and neither did the governmental rulers at the time.

The Roman governor, Pontius Pilate, tried to get some clarity on that issue when Jesus was brought before him. He asked Jesus if he was the king of the Jews. The governor was trying to determine Jesus' political ambition.

"Then Jesus answered, 'I am not an earthly king. If I were, my followers would have fought when I was arrested by the Jewish leaders. But my Kingdom is not of the world'" (John 18:36 TLB). This further confused Pilate. Jesus was not an earthly king? *What other kind of king is there?* the governor probably wondered. *He has a kingdom, but it's not of this world? How odd.*

It is odd unless you understand Jesus' concept of the kingdom. His kingdom was not about toppling the Roman Empire. His opposition wasn't the Romans or even the Jewish leaders. His opposition was Satan, his archenemy. When Adam and Eve sinned, Satan moved in and took over this present world, turning it into a kingdom of darkness. The disciple John said "the world around us is under the control of the evil one" (1 John 5:19).

God, in his goodness, could not allow Satan to rule and ruin the creation he had in the beginning pronounced to be good. He saw this world as a stolen kingdom temporarily under the rule of an enemy whose control would one day come to an end. When Jesus entered human history two thousand years ago, he put Satan on notice that the kingdom he had stolen and enslaved was going to be rescued and reclaimed by the kingdom of heaven. He now leads what we might call a resistance movement against the usurper. This means two warring kingdoms now exist on the earth—the kingdom of this world, ruled by Satan, and the displaced kingdom of heaven ruled by Jesus. When we become Christians, we enlist in Jesus' war to reestablish his kingdom.

So the conflict isn't really political in nature, as Pilate assumed. It isn't even a cultural conflict. The primary enemy isn't wicked people or evil regimes of this world. The war is between God and his ways and Satan and his ways. Yes, we are in a war, but as the apostle Paul said, "We are not fighting against people made of flesh and blood, but against persons without bodies—the evil rulers of the unseen world, those mighty satanic beings and great evil princes of darkness who rule this world; and against huge numbers of wicked spirits in the spirit world" (Ephesians 6:12 TLB). When we live out Jesus' kingdom worldview, we strike a mighty blow in that spiritual conflict. We display the banner of Christ in our own lives, showing the world that his kingdom has already gained ground. He now rules in our hearts and minds, and when he establishes his coming universal rule, we will inherit a place in his eternal kingdom in which his children will love and worship him as the one true God and share in all the goodness and glory of his universal domain for all eternity.

I PLEDGE ALLEGIANCE TO...

As Christians, we are obligated to obey the laws of the land (Romans 13:1–7). Yet when laws violate our moral conscience, we face a conflicting choice.

In one of their many attempts to trap Jesus, the Pharisees asked him whether they should pay taxes to Caesar. Jesus, after showing them a Roman coin bearing the emperor's image and inscription, answered, "Give to Caesar what belongs to Caesar, and give to God what belongs to God" (Matthew 22:21). The wisdom of his reply left them amazed.

Part of the reason Jesus' answer amazed them was that he saw beyond the surface issue and went to the heart of the matter. The real issue then, as it is now, is a question of how a follower of Christ is to live in two kingdoms. For that is what we are called to do. Jesus said in his prayer in John 17, that his followers are "*in* this world" (v. 11) but "do not *belong* to the world" (v. 14). In other words, we live in a kingdom that is ruled by God's enemy, "the ruler of this world" (John 12:31), but "we are citizens of heaven" (Philippians 3:20). As Christians, we hold dual citizenship. We are temporary citizens of the country in which we now live, which is part of an enemy kingdom, and we are permanent citizens of the kingdom of God.

Two different kingdoms. Two different sets of moral standards. In many cases, those standards are similar enough that living in two kingdoms poses no serious problem. In other cases, however, we find the two sets of standards diametrically opposed—with us in the middle.

In Romans Paul clearly states, "Everyone must submit to governing authorities. For all authority comes from God, and those in positions of authority have been placed there by God" (Romans 13:1). Elsewhere, however, the apostle Peter says, "We must obey God rather than any human authority" (Acts 5:29).

These two verses instruct us to be law-abiding citizens of whatever country we live in *to the extent that the law of the land does not contradict the greater law of God.* For instance, we should stop at stop signs, drive according to the speed limit, pay our taxes, and obey the laws established for our good and protection. But if a law of the land orders us to do something that God's Word prohibits— like suppressing the gospel because it is an "intolerant" message that proclaims moral standards the culture rejects—what do we do? The apostles serve as our example. After the Jewish religious authorities warned the apostles to keep quiet about Jesus being the Messiah, they "continued to teach and preach this message: 'Jesus is the Messiah'" (Acts 5:42). They had to choose to follow the command of God or the command of the earthly authorities, and they faced persecution for taking a stand for Christ.

Like the apostles, we are to join in Christ's mission of "reconciling people to him" (2 Corinthians 5:18). Most of us in Western countries haven't experienced the kind of persecution the early Christians faced as they advanced Christ's kingdom within their own culture and to other regions of the world. Christians over the centuries have had their freedoms restricted, endured hardships, and experienced persecution and even death for their faith in Christ.

If you haven't been persecuted for your faith or experienced an attempt to limit your freedom of religion, you have, no doubt, heard of cases in which it has recently happened. When the religious freedom of fellow Christians is repressed, or when they are accused of being bigoted and intolerant, we all suffer. All Christians are part of the body of Christ, and as such "all members care for each other. If one part suffers, all the parts suffer" (1 Corinthians 12:25–26). As members of Christ's body, we must band together and support those who experience a loss of religious freedom or suffer at the hands of an intolerant culture.

HOW DO WE RESPOND?

Your moral beliefs will no doubt be tested in the days ahead. Your position on Christ's claim to be the only way to God, your belief on what constitutes immorality, and your belief about God's design for marriage have become topics of discussion. You may feel some heat, especially from those who want to redefine what marriage is and what it means.

A ruling by the Division of Human Rights (DHR) in New York, for instance, fined a wedding venue $13,000 for refusing to host a lesbian wedding. The DHR ruled the owners of Liberty Ridge Farms in Schaghticoke, New York, violated the state's anti-discrimination law. The owners' constitutional rights to free speech and religious freedom were no defense, according to the ruling. Liberty Ridge Farms paid the fine and has stopped booking ceremonies.[1]

The Colorado Civil Rights Commission upheld an earlier ruling, which found that Masterpiece Cakeshop owner Jack Phillips had discriminated against a gay couple when he denied their request for a wedding cake. Phillips said he had "no problem with preparing cakes and other sweets for lesbians, gay, bisexual, and transgender (LGBT) customers in other circumstances." He further clarified, "I don't feel that I should participate in their wedding, and when I do a cake, I feel like I'm participating in the ceremony or the event or the celebration that the cake is for."[2] Again the owner's defense of a constitutional right of freedom of speech or religion did not hold up in Colorado's court of law. He has since vowed to stop making wedding cakes altogether.

What happens when the biblical narrative about the truth of marriage opposes the cultural narrative? The culture and the courts, it appears, are not going to be tolerant of your moral convictions or your biblical definition of marriage regardless of what the First Amendment says about your religious freedom.

I (Sean) have not shied away from the marriage issue. As I indicated before, I coauthored a book with John Stonestreet entitled *Same-Sex Marriage: A Thoughtful Approach to God's Design for Marriage*. In it we defend the biblical definition of marriage and provide a clear understanding of the specific issues facing us today. Take advantage of resources like this. Be ready and equipped mentally and spiritually when you are challenged or attacked by the proponents of cultural tolerance who are intolerant of any variation from their stance on the marriage issue.

The following excerpt from the book *Same-Sex Marriage* summarizes six steps we all can take that can make a real difference in the same-sex marriage debate.

1. *We can change our reputation from those who hate gays to those who love them.*

We must, of course, speak our convictions about marriage and sexual fidelity whenever necessary, and we know that even when we speak in love and grace, we risk cultural ire. But the truth is, "The church's anti-homosexual reputation isn't just a reputation for opposing gay sex or gay marriage; it's a reputation for hostility to gay people." We can argue about whether the reputation is deserved or not, but our energy would be better spent working to change it.

It starts with the next person we meet. The reality is that far too often, our claims to love those struggling with sexual identity issues or those trapped in homosexual sin sound hollow if not evidenced by actions. Love is not passive.

2. We must tell the truth about same-sex attraction, homosexual sin, and same-sex marriage.

It's tempting to downplay biblical morality to make Christianity more palatable. But loving others requires that we tell the truth, including, when necessary, their homosexual behavior is a sin. It isn't loving to mislead people and suggest that God approves of any and all sexual behavior. He doesn't.

3. We can stop implying in our words and actions that homosexual sin is worse than all other sexual sins, and that sexual sins are unforgivable.

We live in an age of culture-wide sexual brokenness. As G. K. Chesterton once said, "There are many ways to fall down, but there's only one way to stand up straight." Too often, homosexuality is singled out as "what's wrong with America" while other sexual sins get a wink and a nod.

That is wrong.

There is a unity in God's law, which is portrayed in James 2:10: "For whoever keeps the whole law but fails in one point has become accountable for all of it." Though not all sins are equal, all of us stand equally as sinners and lawbreakers before God. With this in mind, we should have more grace towards those whose struggle is different than our own.

4. *We can defend the religious liberty of all Americans.*

    In several high-profile disputes, gay or lesbian couples have accused private business owners of discrimination in cases that will shape our nation's future on religious liberty. District judges in Colorado, New Mexico, and elsewhere have declared that business owners may not refuse their services for same-sex union ceremonies, even if it violates their deeply held convictions.

    Christians must distinguish between discriminating against a gay person and refusing to participate in certain behaviors. Christians should never refuse services to someone because they identify as gay or lesbian. Our actions are to be based on convictions, not hate.

5. *We can tell better stories about love, sex, marriage, and family.*

    The current crop of cultural storytellers is telling this story as they see it, and it isn't helping our cause. We need pro-marriage artists to engage people at the level of their imagination. We need to hear and see stories that reflect the beauty of lifelong married love in a compelling way. People must see the good of marriage in action.

6. *We need to expect the conversations about marriage and be*

ready for them when they come.

It is maddening when Christian leaders are caught off-guard when asked on national television about same-sex marriage! The question will be asked. The opportunity must be seized to speak the truth in love.

But we can't just offload this responsibility on Christian celebrities and spokespersons. We will be asked too, at our family dinners, in college classes and in dorm rooms, over office small talk, on airplanes and at neighborhood block parties. If not prepared when the questions arise, we will find ourselves choosing silence or compromise.[3]

Instilling within your children the biblical narrative of truth about love, sex, and marriage is important. You no doubt want your children to grow up in a society that cherishes the virtues of honor, integrity, and a loving commitment between a man and woman in marriage. Yet at the same time you and all of us must never forget our Christian priority—"Seek the Kingdom of God above all else, and live righteously, and he will give you everything you need" (Matthew 6:33). God's kingdom is not of this world, and as children of God, ours isn't either. Paul says, "Since you have been raised to new life with Christ, set your sights on the realities of heaven, where Christ sits in the place of honor at God's right hand. Think about the things of heaven, not the things of earth" (Colossians 3:1–2).

If we truly believe that God is sovereign, then we can respond with grace and humility when we are attacked for our faith. We should not be surprised that Christians are increasingly being considered "hateful." Jesus said, "If the world hates you, remember that it hated me first. The world would love you as one of its own if you belonged to it, but you are no longer part of the world. I chose you to come out of the world, so it hates you" (John 15:18–19). Jesus then proceeds to tell his disciples that they should *expect* persecution since he himself was persecuted (v. 20). Let's be sure this hatred comes from the nature of the gospel itself, not how we treat (or *mis*treat) people. Nevertheless, if we expect to be mistreated and hated, since we follow a crucified Savior who was rejected by the world, we can respond with much more grace and cheerfulness. In fact, rather than despairing, we should see the current state of Western culture as an opportunity for the gospel to shine in an increasingly dark place.

Perhaps the most helpful biblical model for our times is Daniel. When Judah was exiled to Babylon, Nebuchadnezzar selected Daniel and a few of his friends to come train in his courts for three years so they could "enter the royal service" (Daniel 1:5). This was a great privilege and honor for Daniel, but there was one problem— the king had ordered them to eat nonkosher food. Nevertheless, "Daniel was determined not to defile himself by eating the food and wine given to them by the king" (Daniel 1:8). Instead of giving in, and facing potential harsh consequences, Daniel thought of a creative alternative, which involved allowing himself and his friends to go on a special diet for ten days and then having their health tested. Their plan worked and God blessed the young men with wisdom, skill in literature, and understanding in dreams and visions (v. 17).

We live in times not too unlike Babylon. Our surrounding culture seems increasingly at odds with biblical morality. And we find ourselves facing unforeseen challenges not only in our personal relationships, but also at times with the government. How can we respond? We certainly don't pretend to have all the answers in this book. But we believe Daniel teaches us two powerful principles. First, we must not compromise our moral convictions, even if it costs us personally. Many times the demonstration of biblical love turns out well. Many times it doesn't. Daniel did not know how the story would end. He could have been given a fate like John the Baptist or Stephen. But regardless, he was willing to stand on principle and let the "chips fall where they may." Second, we need to think creatively. Daniel thought outside the box and offered a creative solution to a seemingly recalcitrant dilemma. We find ourselves in unforeseen difficulties for which there are rarely simple answers. We need to pray to God for wisdom and creativity (James 1:5).

Even though we don't belong to this earthly kingdom, we still must live in it and engage in the business and activities going on around us—and that includes countering cultural tolerance. Yet the very fact that we are first seeking God's kingdom enables us to be more effective in being God's salt and light right here on earth. In concluding this chapter, we leave you with a poignant quote from C. S. Lewis, who makes this point so very clear.

If you read history, you will find that the Christians who did most for the present world were just those who thought most about the next. The apostles themselves, who set on foot the conversion of the Roman Empire, the great men who built up the Middle Ages, the English Evangelicals who abolished the Slave Trade, all left their mark on Earth, precisely because their minds were occupied with heaven. It is since Christians have largely ceased to think of the other world that they have become so ineffective in this. Aim at heaven and you will get earth "thrown in": Aim at earth and you will get neither.[4]

CHAPTER 10

CULTURAL TOLERANCE AND SOCIETY

Short of total isolation, the American society you live in today is going to influence how your children make moral choices in one way or another. Stop and think about it. What are the voices of society telling your children about the choices they are about to make? What is the central theme that today's culture emphasizes over and over again? If you were to reduce it to a single sentence, it might look like this: *You have the right to choose for yourself what is right for you and what is wrong for you—and no one should judge that choice.*

We see and hear it expressed in so many ways in the arts, in literature, in entertainment, in the whole of our society: "You are the captain of your own fate. You choose what's right for you. No one has the right to judge you for the moral choices you make. It's in your hands—you decide what is true and moral for you." That message is reinforced over and over again until most of our young people have bought into it.

The doctrine of cultural tolerance is built on the foundation of individual supremacy. It is the individual who determines what is best for him or her. Each person must determine what is right and wrong for himself or herself. And the culture will be intolerant of any person or group who suggests there is a morality outside ourselves that judges another person's choices.

This erroneous claim that we are the arbiters of our own morality has far-reaching ramifications. To decide for ourselves what is moral and right sets us up as our own gods and puts us in opposition to the true God who alone is the author and arbiter of morality. Inevitably, moral choices based on our own moral compass will often be wrong choices. And wrong moral choices can result in consequences ranging from minor disappointments to major disasters emotionally, relationally, physically, and spiritually.

CHALLENGE THEIR THINKING

Moving our young people toward the biblical narrative about moral truth is often best done by challenging their thinking about what makes our actions and attitudes right or wrong in the first place. This will inevitably lead them back to why the person and character of God is the only true standard for deciding what is morally right and wrong.

When I (Sean) was a teenager, my dad challenged my thinking about moral truth. He often used current events and movies to guide my reasoning. I have done the same with my own children.

On one occasion he took me, my girlfriend (who became my wife), and my sister to see Steven Spielberg's *Schindler's List*. It seemed everyone was talking about it. It won seven Academy Awards, including the awards for Best Picture and Best Director. The movie was based on a true story about a German businessman named Oskar Schindler who saved the lives of more than a thousand mostly Polish-Jewish refugees during the Nazi Holocaust.

As we left the theater, we were surrounded by a somber crowd, many of whom were commenting on the atrocities inflicted on the Jews by the Nazis.

My dad turned to me and asked, "Sean, do you believe the Holocaust was wrong—morally wrong?"

I answered quickly. "Yes, of course."

Then, as we got into the car to travel to a restaurant, he pursued the matter with all three of us. "Almost everyone walking out of that theater would say the Holocaust was wrong," he explained. "But what basis would they have for making that judgment? Could they answer *why* it was wrong?"

The "Why is it wrong?" question really got me to thinking. I remember saying it's wrong because the Bible says so. But then my dad asked me why the Bible says it's wrong. I was speechless and really had no idea. Dad continued, "Most people in America subscribe to a view of morality called 'cultural ethics.' In other words, they believe that whatever is acceptable in that culture is moral; if the majority of people say a thing is right, then it is right."

We arrived at the restaurant, and Dad continued to make his point. "That's why many Americans will say that abortion is okay, because the majority of Americans—and Congress and the Supreme Court—have accepted it. If the majority thinks it's okay, it must be okay, right?"

"But there's a problem with that," he explained. "If that is true, then how can we say the 'aborting' of six million Jews in the Holocaust was wrong? In fact, the Nazis offered that very argument as a defense at the Nuremberg Trials. They argued, 'How can you come from another culture and condemn what we did when we acted according to what our culture said was acceptable?' In condemning them, the tribunal said that there is something beyond culture, above culture, that determines right and wrong."

He also went on to explain that most of what people call morality today is simply pragmatism. "*If we don't condemn what the Nazis did,* people reason within themselves, *what's to stop someone from doing it to us?* And they're right, of course," he told us. "They recognize the need for objective morality, but they can't arrive at a true moral code—because they refuse to acknowledge the original."

Finally, after about two hours of discussion, Dad pressed in on the first question he posed. He looked straight at me, probably because I was the oldest. "Do you know *why* what you saw tonight was wrong?"

"I know it was wrong," I ventured, "but I guess I don't know why it was wrong."

"There is a truth," he said, "that is outside you and all of us, above our family, and beyond any human—a truth about murder that originates in the person of God. Murder is wrong because there is a God, and that God is the giver and preserver of life. When he created the first human he said, 'It is good,' and commanded us to protect life and not to commit murder."

That night I grasped the truth that God is the original life-giver and is the one with authority over life—he has the right to give life and to take life. *Schindler's List* gave my dad an ideal opportunity to help me, my girlfriend, and my sister to understand that without God as the standard, there can be no universal moral guidelines.

This same reasoning applies to all other ethical issues as well. The basis of everything we call moral, the source of every good thing, is the eternal God who is outside us, above us, and beyond us. As we mentioned earlier, lying and stealing are wrong because God is truth (John 14:6). Justice is right because God is just (Genesis 18:25). Hatred is wrong because God is love (1 John 4:8). Forgiveness is right because God is mercy (Ephesians 2:4). Sexual immorality is wrong because God is faithful and pure (Deuteronomy 7:9). These things are right or wrong, not because society or even the church agrees with them or frowns on them, but because they are either contrary to or consistent with the nature and character of God.

THE 4-CS PROCESS

A couple years after I (Josh) discussed *Schindler's List* with Sean, Stephanie, and my daughter Katie, I launched the "Right from Wrong" Campaign. During that time my publishing team worked with me to create an easy-to-use process to teach young people how to determine what is morally right and distinguish it from wrong. We called it the "4-Cs Process." Hundreds of thousands of families have used it and still use it to help their children determine what is truly right and what is truly wrong. I have continued to share this process in my speaking and published materials. Recently I included them in a book to dads titled *10 Commitments for Dads*.[1]

I will draw on that book to make applying the process of determining right from wrong as practical as possible. Let's call on Todd and his son Chad to illustrate the 4-Cs Process for us. Chad has been caught shoplifting, and his parents are confronting him about it. But to Chad, it really isn't a big deal. He even feels he was justified in doing what he did. Let's see how Todd and his wife, Laura, handle the situation. First, we will show them reacting as many parents would, and then we will re-create the situation and show them walking Chad through the 4-Cs Process.

"Chad, I promised you that this wouldn't be like all those other 'talks' we've had," Todd began. "I honestly don't want to yell at you anymore."

Silence descended quickly on the room, punctuated by a sniffle from Laura, Chad's mother. Todd and Laura were confronting their son, who had been arrested for shoplifting at the local electronics store.

"I just want some answers," Todd continued. He began to draw his son out, asking questions.

"How do you feel after being arrested for shoplifting?"

"I don't know."

"Do you feel guilty?"

"No."

"Because you don't think it's wrong?"

"No, it's not that, exactly. I guess maybe I feel sorta bad in a way."

"Why?"

"I don't know."

"Don't you know what you did was wrong?" Laura chimed in. As she looked at Chad, she realized that at times her son seemed like a stranger to her. At other times, she could still see the little boy who would crawl up on her lap as she read him bedtime stories.

"Why do you guys think it's so wrong?" Chad asked.

Todd flashed him a puzzled look. "What do you mean?"

"Why is it so wrong? I took one measly camera, that's all. The last video camera I got from them never did work right. They owed me another camera but wouldn't give it to me. What's so wrong about taking what's owed you?"

"I can't believe this!" Todd said.

Chad rolled his eyes. He slumped back against the couch and crossed his arms.

"Chad," Laura answered, "your father and I have tried to teach you honesty from day one. And it is so disappointing that you can't see that stealing is wrong."

"Who's stealing?" Chad snapped. "I'm sure not. That store is the one stealing from the pockets of its customers every day. They're the ones who need to be arrested."

Todd was beginning to lose his temper. "You know good and well you had no right to take that camera, no matter what the store does to their customers. We've taught you better than that, Chad David!"

Laura, seated beside Todd, responded to the anger in her husband's voice by pressing on his arm firmly.

"Look," she said, in a calming voice. "Taking something from a store without paying for it is wrong, regardless of their business practices."

"Why?" Chad persisted.

"What do you mean, 'Why?'" Todd shot back. "It's wrong! Some things are just wrong, dead wrong. And you and I both know what you did was wrong."

Chad's voice rose in reaction. "Well, you may think it's wrong, but I don't. You're entitled to your opinion, and I'm entitled to mine. None of my friends think I did a thing wrong. The one in the wrong here is that store." He rose from the couch and began walking out of the room.

"You get back here right now, young man," Todd demanded.

"I've got to get ready for soccer," he announced from the top of the stairway.

Laura pressed Todd on the arm again. "You promised him this 'talk' would be different." Todd leaned back in his chair, closed his eyes, and wondered how his boy's moral compass had gotten so far off the mark.

Todd and Laura want what every Christian parent wants—we all want our children to believe that certain things are right and other things are wrong so they can make right moral choices in life. Chad's parents know their son has made the wrong choice but feel helpless to convince him otherwise. It is this feeling of helplessness that often drives us to lash out inappropriately and be confused about what to do. That's when we are most likely to get angry or frustrated. Realizing and acknowledging this is a good first step. Such acknowledgment might have helped Todd respond more compassionately.

It's not that Chad doesn't know instinctively that some things are right and some things are wrong. Let him discover, for example, that his soccer shoes were stolen from his school locker and he'll feel wronged. He wouldn't argue that the thief is entitled to his opinion of right and wrong; he would appeal to an objective sense of justice by claiming that he had suffered an injustice. In so doing, of course, he would be appealing to a moral law that he believes everyone—not just he—ought to follow.

In Chad's opinion, his actions were justified because the electronics store didn't treat him or other people fairly. So in effect his "moral law" made it okay to steal. In fact, many of our young people today believe it's okay to steal, lie, or cheat depending on the circumstances. According to them, what is wrong in one situation may be right in another.

Although it may not be the natural inclination, it is important for parents to see experiences like these as opportunities to teach their children to truly understand right and wrong. Many parents get insecure and afraid at the wrong behavior of their children. As a result, some become legalistic and only care about "sin avoidance" rather than the development of genuinely good moral character. Stealing is never good. And consequences do have to be paid. But if parents see instances like these as opportunities to help their children truly understand right from wrong, and to experience grace firsthand, they will have the best chance of seeing them develop Christlike character.

That is where God becomes an essential part of the discussion— because it is impossible to arrive at an objective and universal standard of morality without him in the picture. The 4-Cs Process was designed to help you include God in the discussion when dealing with matters of morality with your children.

Let's recreate the situation with Chad and his parents and, using the 4-Cs Process, learn what they could have done to help their son determine how taking from even a disreputable electronics store was wrong.

THE 4-CS PROCESS IS MADE UP OF FOUR DECISION-MAKING STEPS:

1. *Consider* the choice.
2. *Compare* it to God.
3. *Commit* to God's way.
4. *Count* on God's protection and provision.

1. Consider the Choice.

In a single day, each of us makes literally scores of choices. Most of them are almost automatic. We choose what time to get up in the morning, what clothes to wear, what to eat, what route to take to work or school, where to park, and so on. We take little time or thought in considering these choices.

But when it comes to moral choices, we need to pause and realize we are at a crossroads. The choices we make—to be less than honest, to advance a flirtation to the next level, or as a student, to enhance our score by "borrowing" someone else's answers—are often made without considering the gravity of what we are really doing. To make right moral choices, we must first pause long enough to remind ourselves that we are facing a right or wrong decision.

Let's assume Chad had told his parents about the video camera he bought and the store's refusal to make it right. How could Todd and Laura have used the 4-Cs Process to guide their son to the realization that taking a camera, even from a less-than-reputable store, was still wrong?

"I took the camera back, Dad, and they won't do anything to

fix it unless they charge me," Chad laments. "They say I must have messed it up, but I didn't. I feel like taking a new camera when they're not looking so I can replace this crummy one. They've gotta pay somehow."

"You're right, son," Todd responds, "they are not doing right by you. But you need to pause a minute to realize this is a time to consider the choice. There is a right decision to make here and a wrong one. And you want to make the right choice, because choices do have consequences."

2. Compare It to God.

Chad's failure was in neglecting to compare his attitude and action to the character of God. This would have meant looking at the choice in relation to God's commands to be honest, which are in Chad's best interest. Of course, before this comparison could affect Chad positively, it would be necessary for him to believe that God, not himself, is the universal standard for right.

Using this approach, Chad's parents could have said something like the following:

"Chad, I know it doesn't seem fair. The store sold you a defective camera, and they won't make it right. They are, in fact, being dishonest with you."

"You're right, Mom. For once you guys are really right."

Laura and Todd laughed, and Laura continued. "We could say since the store won't own up to their dishonesty, we are justified in making them own up—we can then take what is properly ours, right?"

"Right on," Chad replied. "And besides, they've got so many cameras they won't even miss it if I lift one from them."

"This all may sound good on the surface," Todd said. "But

what you would be doing is justifying your actions based on what *you* think is right, rather than looking to God, who defines what honesty and dishonesty really are."

What Todd and Laura were doing here was directing their son to the original standard for what constitutes honesty. Chad was rationalizing that it wasn't actually dishonest to steal from someone who owes another person. But when we take it on ourselves to rationalize in this way, we are actually usurping God's rightful role as the sovereign arbiter. The Bible says:

- "Do not steal.
- "Do not lie.
- "Do not deceive one another. . . .
- "Do not defraud or rob your neighbor." (Leviticus 19:11–13 NIV)

God's commands to be honest come out of his nature, and his nature is true and right. Scripture says that "even if everyone else is a liar, God is true" (Romans 3:4). By his very nature he is a God of integrity, and because of this "it is impossible for God to lie" (Hebrews 6:18). He is sovereign; he is the one who defines what is right and what is wrong regarding honesty and every other moral action. When we make our moral decision in light of the character of God, our choice becomes crystal clear—in this example, we are to commit to being honest even when we are wronged by a dishonest business.

3. Commit to God's Way.

Committing to God's way is easier said than done. It means we have to admit we are not the ruler over our lives—he is. As we said before, the concept behind cultural tolerance is that you have the right to decide what is "right for you." People find that highly appealing because it puts them in charge. It permits them to justify their attitudes and actions and disregard how they compare with God's character. Granting ourselves the capacity to decide our own morality makes us feel independent and empowering. And that temptation is not easy to resist.

"Chad, you may feel that justice was served when you took that camera from the store," Todd continued. "But it's never just to go against God's standard of honesty. Taking what you feel is rightfully yours while the store isn't looking would be deceitful, which is as wrong as stealing. You would, in effect, be setting yourself up as judge, jury, and executioner. But God says that is his role: 'It is mine to avenge; I will repay' (Deuteronomy 32:35 NIV). He tells us to 'not seek revenge or bear a grudge'" (Leviticus 19:18).

"But, Dad, it's still not fair," Chad protested.

"You're right; it's not fair," Todd agreed. "But there are things in life that are not fair that we must leave in God's hands. Jesus, for example, was certainly treated unfairly, yet the Bible says, 'He did not retaliate when he was insulted, nor threaten revenge when he suffered. He left his case in the hands of God, who always judges fairly' " (1 Peter 2:23).

"And," Laura added, "you can count on it—God will honor you for doing the right thing and leaving it up to him to deal with the electronics store."

4. Count on God's Protection and Provision.

When we humbly admit God's sovereignty and lovingly seek to please him, not only can we begin to see clearly the distinctions between right and wrong, but we can also begin to count on his protection and provision.

This doesn't mean that everything will be rosy; in fact, God says bluntly that we may suffer for righteousness' sake. But even such suffering has rewards. Living according to his way brings many spiritual blessings, like freedom from guilt, a clear conscience, and knowing our actions please him.

We can also enjoy many physical, emotional, psychological, and relational benefits when we commit to God's ways. Of course, his protection and provision should not be the primary motivation for obeying him; we should obey him simply because we love him and trust him. But the practical and spiritual benefits of obedience certainly provide powerful encouragement for choosing right and rejecting wrong.

Todd and Laura had the opportunity to help Chad realize that adhering to God's standard of honesty would bring protection and provision to him on at least four levels. Aligning ourselves with God's standard of honesty provides the following benefits:

- protects us from guilt and provides a clear conscience and an uninterrupted relationship with God
- protects us from shame and provides a sense of accomplishment
- protects us from the cycle of deceit and provides a reputation of integrity
- protects us from ruined relationships and provides trusting relationships

The secret to making right choices in life is having the deep conviction that God always has your best interest at heart. Instill within your children that he is a good God who loves them beyond their comprehension. And when they believe that with their whole heart, they can obey his commands to be honest, live sexually pure, love and respect others, show mercy, forgive, exhibit self-control, and so on. Being obedient isn't simply a matter of adhering to obligation and duty—it comes from a "God who is jealous about his relationship with [them]" (Exodus 34:14). Embrace that truth in your own life—and instill it in the life of your children.[2]

And realize that while loving God's laws gives us a desire to obey, being united to Christ is what gives us the *power* to do so. Paul explains:

> *For if we have been united with him in a death like his, we shall certainly be united with him in a resurrection like his. We know that our old self was crucified with him in order that the body of sin might be brought to nothing, so that we would no longer be enslaved to sin. For one who has died has been set free from sin. Now if we have died with Christ, we believe that we will also live with him. We know that Christ, being raised from the dead, will never die again; death no longer has dominion over him. For the death he died he died to sin, once for all, but the life he lives he lives to God. So you also must consider yourselves dead to sin and alive to God in Christ Jesus.*
>
> *Let not sin therefore reign in your mortal body, to make you obey its passions. Do not present your members to sin as instruments for unrighteousness, but present yourselves to God as those who have been brought from death to life, and your members to God as instruments for righteousness. For sin will have no dominion over you, since you are not under law but under grace. (Romans 6:5–14 ESV)*

In Romans 8:1–17, Paul explains that the same Spirit who gave Christ life gives us life as well. It is the Spirit who gives us hope and power for living in a way that honors God. The Spirit allows us to "put to death the deeds of the body" (v.14). If we are united with Christ, the Spirit lives within us. We have died to sin and have been raised up with Christ in the power of the Spirit, and we are being conformed to the image of the Creator. We can rest in the security that Christ's righteousness has covered our sins and that we have grace. We need to remember these realities and live in accordance with them. When your child knows that, he or she is freed to obey without fear and anxiety.

The doctrine of cultural tolerance has permeated our society. It will take a very intentional and concerted effort on your part to counter its influence. Hopefully you can look to your church pastor and youth worker for excellent support. However, even the church has been negatively affected by cultural tolerance. How that has happened in many churches, possibly your own, and what you can do about it is the topic of the next chapter.

CHAPTER 11

CULTURAL TOLERANCE AND THE CHURCH

Your children's lives are inundated with technology. According to a Kaiser Family Foundation study "today's teens spend more than 7½ hours a day consuming media—watching TV, listening to music, surfing the Web, social networking, and playing video games."[1] More than three-quarters of them own a cell phone and text an average of sixty times a day.

With full schedules and all the technological distractions, most parents are finding it increasingly difficult to connect with their children in meaningful ways. A Pew Research study found that "over half (53%) of all working parents with children under age 18 say it is difficult for them to balance the responsibilities of their job with the responsibilities of their family."[2] Of this group, 40 percent of mothers and 34 percent of fathers say they always feel rushed.[3]

Instilling biblical morality in our children takes time, energy, and wisdom. We need all the help we can get. Many turn to resources, like this book, for help. Many more turn to their church for support. Certainly the church should be a strong source of help in countering the influence of cultural tolerance in the life of our young people.

FIVE MISCONCEPTIONS FUEL CULTURAL TOLERANCE IN THE CHURCH

You may attend a church that shares your values, teaches that the Bible is God's Word, and reinforces biblical morality in the lives of your children. What many don't realize, however, is how the doctrine of cultural tolerance is often unwittingly fueled within the church, even among church attendees, because of certain misconceptions about the Bible. We don't mean it's likely that your church is openly teaching that the Bible isn't the inspired Word of God or suggesting that moral truth is relative and subjectively determined. Nor is it likely they are insisting that you endorse other people's beliefs or lifestyle choices. Yet church leadership and those who teach our young people must remain vigilant so error does not creep into how we understand universal truth and scripture.

Scripture is the foundation of all we believe about God, ourselves, and the world around us. How we view God's Word, what we believe it is, and how we interpret it and apply it to our lives is critical. There are four statements about scripture that represent many Christians' view of the Bible. What they don't realize is how cultural tolerance gets a foothold in the church and is reinforced within our young people' lives when we maintain certain misconceptions about truth and God's Word. Just a little error mixed with truth can reinforce the doctrine of cultural tolerance. Examine the following statements. Do you sense they are completely true or only partially true?

1. The Old and New Testaments are the Bible of the Jewish and Christian faiths.
2. The Bible contains truth designed just for me.
3. There are 101 ways to interpret the Bible.
4. What's true for you isn't necessarily true for me.
5. The Bible is God's Word, but experience determines interpretation.

Some or all of these statements may seem right to you. Each of them is true to an extent, yet each of them contains an element of error or is only partially true. Let's take each of these statements and learn from them how misconceptions about universal truth and the Bible within the church perpetuate the idea that all truth claims are equal and subjectively created.

1. The Old and New Testaments are the Bible of the Jewish and Christian Faiths.

It is true that the Jewish faith finds its roots in the Hebrew text (Old Testament). And the Bible of the Christian faith includes both the New Testament and the Old Testament. The problem is not that these statements are not true; it is that the current culture thinks of the Bible as relevant only within the scope of the two religions that spring from it. They see it as a sort of handbook laying out the rules and regulations for two particular religions. Just as a lodge or a club or a service organization such as Lions or Kiwanis has its own handbook of rules that apply only to them, so the Christians and Jews have their handbook outlining the goals and bylaws of their religions. The fallacy with this view is that it directly infers that Christianity is merely one religion among others that are also equally valid.

What the culture does not grasp is that the Bible is not a book exclusively for Jews and Christians. If we believe that is all the Bible is—just a religious book—then we propagate the notion that these ancient writings represent two among many equally valid and true religions. But the Bible is far more than the basis for a religion.

The Bible is the revelation of God, the Creator of all things, to the human race. It is not merely a religious book for a specific religion. It is Creator God's words and thoughts revealed to a select group of men that put into writing what he wanted them to say. These men brought their own unique abilities and personalities to the writing task but ultimately were inspired by God. That is what the apostle Paul meant when he wrote, "All Scripture is inspired by God" (2 Timothy 3:16). The word "inspired" is translated from the Greek word *theopneustos*, which literally means "God-breathed."

The apostle Peter referred to the inspiration of God's Word like this: "No prophecy in Scripture ever came from the prophet's own understanding, or from human initiative. No, those prophets were moved by the Holy Spirit, and they spoke from God" (2 Peter 1:20–21). Each book, each page, and each paragraph of scripture was written in a specific human context, yet because the Spirit of God worked through the writers, it still communicates the exact message God wants all of creation to receive. The Bible is the message of God reaching out to a fallen and lost human race in an effort to redeem and restore humans to a relationship with him—*all* humans, not just those of a particular religion.

The doctrine of cultural tolerance would limit the Bible to being a religious book solely for the Jewish and Christian religions—just one religious book among many. To counter this, speak of scripture to your family and friends as the revelation of God to the entire world. It reveals to all humans who he is, what he is like, who we all are, why we are here, why we are separated from him, and how we—his lost creation—can be redeemed from our fatal alienation from him and enjoy a relationship with him throughout eternity. Also, in today's skeptical culture, it is important to be prepared to give good historical, scientific, and philosophical evidences for why the Bible, among all religious texts, is uniquely the Word of God.

The Bible presents a view of life very different from how humans see it. It presents God's view of the world—his worldview, to be exact. (A *worldview* is what we assume to be true about the basic makeup of our world.) And it is his worldview that God wants every person, from every culture of the world, from ages past to the present to the end of time, to understand and embrace. The Bible is no ordinary book. Reverence it, read it, and represent it to your family as the life-giving words to all the world from the "God who is jealous about his relationship with you" (Exodus 34:14).

2. The Bible Contains Truth Designed Just for Me.

There is no question that God speaks directly to us through his inspired Word. At times his truth is very specific in its application to us and often comes at a time we need it most. God undoubtedly must have designed it for each of us at just the right moment of our lives. This view is not necessarily an incorrect one. It can have implications, however, that fuel the idea that moral truth is subjective.

Imagine you are seated in a small group Bible study. Gary, the leader, has just finished reading 2 Peter 1:3–4 to the group. He turns to Marci, who is sitting right next to you, and asks, "What do these verses mean?"

Marci, a professed Christian, pauses to reflect on the passage. "Well," she begins, "what these verses mean to *me* is that God is there to help me live the Christian life." Gary nods and says, "That's good." He looks right at you. "What do these verses mean to *you?*"

Chances are you wouldn't even detect the subtle shift in meaning between Gary's first question to Marci and then his question to you after Marci's response. But look again. The importance of the words "means to me" and "mean to you" should not be overlooked. They are indicative of the influence of cultural tolerance. Rather than looking to the biblical text in order to know *the objective* truth, many Christians are actually looking for *their subjective* meaning of the truth.

This is not to minimize the importance of applying scriptural truth to our lives—it is imperative that we do so. However, it is very important to understand that each book of the Bible conveys a specific truth that is objective and true whether or not we capture its application to our lives. In fact, biblical application depends on understanding the objective meaning of the text. God wants us to discover the meaning of his truth and then experience that truth as our own.

Coming to scripture to discover God's meaning shifts the focus away from a merely subjective experience to an objective standard of truth derived from the person of God. Ultimately, God wants us to discover him, know him for who he is, and enjoy an eternal relationship with him (John 17:1–5). Maintaining that focus is important. It will help keep you from falling into the error of thinking that truth is subjectively created by the individual. It will center you on the idea that we are to discover God's original intended meaning of his truth and then apply that truth to life.

3. There Are 101 Ways to Interpret the Bible.

If moral truth is a matter of opinion and subjectively determined, as proponents of cultural tolerance claim, then it stands to reason there are as many ways to interpret the Bible as there are people. One church will interpret a certain passage one way while another church will interpret the same passage another way. A TV preacher will expound on a set of verses and say it means this, and another will claim those verses mean something else entirely. There certainly are many ways to interpret the Bible. And with many good pastors and churches interpreting verses differently, can there really be an objective meaning to the text?

The apostle Peter wrote that, "no prophecy of Scripture is a matter of one's own interpretation" (2 Peter 1:20 NASB). Therefore, we must be careful not to inject our personal views into scripture but rather seek out God's intended meaning. This is the difference between *exegesis* (finding the objective meaning of a biblical text) and *eisegesis* (reading subjective meaning into the biblical text). As much as we may want to understand how a scriptural truth applies to our own lives, we must remember that the Bible was not written directly to us who live in Western civilization in the the twenty-first century.

The Old Testament was written to the nation of Israel. When Jesus spoke to his disciples, the crowds, and various individuals, he was speaking to those who lived in the nation of Israel in the first century. Each writer of the books of the Bible had a certain audience in mind. It's unlikely that these writers foresaw that, thousands of years later, their writings would be published as the authoritative Holy Bible for the entire human race.

But even though these men wrote within their own specific historical contexts to audiences considerably different from those in the world today, and even though the words of scripture may not have been written specifically *to* us in the twenty-first century, it doesn't mean they weren't written *for* us. The authors of scripture wrote *to* a specific audience, yet the truth of those writings is nonetheless *for* the entire world. The immediate context and application of a given truth may have been specific to a particular time and circumstance, but ultimately the truth of God's Word transcends history, culture, customs, languages, and timelines.

The apostle Paul tells us to "be diligent. . .[in] accurately handling the word of truth" (2 Timothy 2:15 NASB). To handle scripture accurately, we must first interpret the meaning of the Bible accurately to understand the truth that God intended for a specific audience within a specific time in history. And then we can determine what application that truth has for us today.

Proper biblical interpretation requires that we avoid the three most common mistakes people make when attempting to interpret scripture. Those mistakes are:

- They take a scripture verse or words out of context.
- They inject their own views into the text.
- They ignore the genre of the text (whether poetry, history, narrative, or apocalyptic).

These errors cause people to misinterpret the meaning and message of God's Word. To correct the first error, we must realize that proper interpretation requires proper context. We can keep scripture within context when we understand the setting of a passage—what comes immediately before a verse and what comes after. When we isolate a verse and fail to understand it within the whole of the narrative, we are in danger of misinterpreting the meaning.

The second error, injecting our own views into a passage, is something all of us are guilty of to a greater or lesser degree. Sometimes people misuse Bible verses just to make their own point or to justify their particular moral stance. It's a pretty handy device for self-justification or rationalization. Ignore context and inject our own meaning into a text and we can make just about any point we want.

The third way to misinterpret scripture is to ignore the genre of the text. The Bible was not only written in different settings and in different times, it was also written in different literary genres. These genres include history, narrative, poetry, prophecy, instruction, and apocalyptic writing. The first seventeen books of the Old Testament, for example, are largely history. But not every historical account is meant to be taken as a model for behavior. Just because the Bible accurately reported things like hatred, fighting, rape, wars, and the like doesn't mean God approved of such things. We must be able to discern the difference between historical reporting and the truths God wants us to learn from the events recorded. As we can see, there is a correct means of interpreting God's Word, which requires careful study.

4. What's True for You Isn't Necessarily True for Me.

Who is to say one theological viewpoint is more right than another? Some Bible-believing Christians are Calvinists while others are Wesleyan-Armenian. Some Christians claim a prayer covering for women is required; others don't. Some Christians praise God with a worship band, while others say musical instruments in the church should be forbidden. These types of differences have led many Christians to say, "What's true for you isn't necessarily true for me."

The natural conclusion of this kind of thinking is that truth must be a matter of opinion. This conclusion reveals a deep-seated confusion between the concepts of *truth* and *belief*.

We are all entitled to our own beliefs, but this doesn't mean each of us has our own truths. Our beliefs describe the way we think the world is. Truth describes the objective state of the world regardless of how we take it to be. Beliefs can be relative, but truth cannot. So when we consider the nature of truth—that it is an objective description of reality—it makes no sense to say that something is true for you and not for me.

For example, imagine you have a frugal son. He places his piggy bank on the table and is about to open it up. You ask him how much he believes is in the bank. He says, "I believe there's more than $20 in there." You counter and say, "*I* believe there is less than $20." Can your varying beliefs about how much the bank contains create two distinct truths? The only way to solve the dispute, of course, is to open the piggy bank and count the money. The instant the money is counted, the truth will be revealed and the false beliefs will be exposed. The truth about the exact dollar amount in the piggy bank exists independently of what you or your son believes about it.

It's the same when it comes to moral truths. God's Word becomes the standard of what is morally true because moral truths stem from God's character, revealed in his Word. These truths declare the way things really are. They are not open to being rewritten as if they were merely personal or subjective viewpoints. What we may believe about moral truths doesn't change whether or not they are true. So while moral truths are not up for consideration as personal or subjective, beliefs can be. Personal beliefs strongly held are often called "personal convictions."

In the book of Romans, the apostle Paul addressed the fact that some Jewish followers of Christ were conflicted over what eating restrictions they should follow, what festival days they should observe, and on what day they should celebrate the Sabbath. He told them that "those who don't eat certain foods must not condemn those who do, for God has accepted them" (Romans 14:3). And concerning what day they should worship on, he said, "You should each be fully convinced that whichever day you choose is acceptable" (Romans 14:5).

Paul essentially was calling for the Christians in Rome to be tolerant of one another in the traditional sense of the word; that is, to graciously accept a difference they disagreed with. Some of the Jewish Christians were still holding on to certain requirements of the Old Testament law and Jewish worship. Paul had already written to the Galatian church that the Jewish law (not the moral law) was no longer needed. "The law was our guardian until Christ came," he wrote. "And now that the way of faith has come, we no longer need the [Jewish] law as our guardian" (Galatians 3:24–25). But for some in Rome, it was a struggle to let go of the old customs.

Paul was appealing to the stronger, more mature Christians to be tolerant of those who were struggling with these issues.

Paul wrote, "We who are strong must be considerate of those who are sensitive about things like this" (Romans 15:1). Ultimately, he asked them to be patient with one another for the sake of unity. "May God, who gives this patience and encouragement," he admonished them, "help you live in complete harmony with each other" (Romans 15:5).

Paul was making the point that there were issues of belief and preference outside of the universal moral law of God that required a personal decision and were between that person and God. Believers needed to be tolerant of each other regarding these choices.

I (Sean) know some people who feel very strongly that to honor the Lord's Day they must refrain from buying products on Sunday. Some people feel it is right to place their children in Christian schools, and it would be wrong for them to enroll their children in public school. Many of these people don't condemn those who do otherwise, but they see these as personal convictions or beliefs they must follow. The apostle Paul made this point quite clear when he referred to the now superseded Jewish regulations on what foods were pure or impure. "I know and am convinced," Paul said, "on the authority of the Lord Jesus that no food, in and of itself, is wrong to eat. But if someone believes it is wrong [for them], then for that person it is wrong" (Romans 14:14).

Paul's primary point is that when someone has a personal conviction on certain disputed issues, he or she should not condemn others for violating his or her particular belief. These types of personal convictions are developed between God and the individual and are not to be imposed on others. Personal conviction should be arrived at after great care, study of scripture, and the wise counsel of other mature Christians.

5. The Bible Is God's Word, but Experience Determines Interpretation.

This final misconception is perhaps the most prevalent example of how cultural tolerance influences the church. In fact, this is the move made by Matthew Vines, author of *God and the Gay Christian: The Biblical Case in Support of Same-Sex Relationships*. He begins his book by affirming the final authority of scripture on questions of morality and doctrine: "Like most theologically conservative Christians, I hold what is often called a 'high view' of the Bible. That means I believe all of Scripture is inspired by God and authoritative for my life. While some parts of the Bible address cultural norms that do not directly apply to modern societies, all of Scripture 'is useful for teaching, for reproof, for correction, and for training in righteousness' (2 Timothy 3:16–17 NRSV)."[4] And yet when Vines discovered his own same-sex attraction, his perspective began to change based on his personal experience. Now he has become an outspoken advocate for LGBT rights within the church, and his goal is to lead a movement to convince Christians that they can affirm the full authority of scripture and also affirm committed, monogamous same-sex relationships.

Vines claims to recognize how important it is that we not elevate our experience over scripture. In fact, he says, "I wasn't asking them [conservative Christians] to revise the Bible based on my experience. I was asking them to reconsider their *interpretation* of the Bible." Fair point. But he continues, "While Scripture tells us not to rely solely on our experience, it also cautions us not to ignore our experience altogether."[5] Vines supports his point with an example from the Sermon on the Mount where Jesus warned against false prophets:

"Beware of false prophets, who come to you in sheep's clothing but inwardly are ravenous wolves. You will recognize them by their fruits. Are grapes gathered from thornbushes, or figs from thistles? So, every healthy tree bears good fruit, but the diseased tree bears bad fruit. A healthy tree cannot bear bad fruit, nor can a diseased tree bear good fruit. Every tree that does not bear good fruit is cut down and thrown into the fire. Thus you will recognize them by their fruits." (Matthew 7:15–20 ESV)

According to Vines, Jesus provides a simple test for a genuine prophet: "If something bears bad fruit, it cannot be a good tree. And if something bears good fruit, it cannot be a bad tree."[6] Since Vines believes traditional Christian teaching on homosexual behavior brings harm to gay people (depression and suicide, for instance) then it must not be biblical. By contrast, embracing monogamous same-sex relationships brings "good fruit" to gay people, and so it must be right.

Since Vines believes this is a question of interpretation, not biblical authority, the question is a matter of what the text *means*. Earlier we stated how important it is to consider context. If you read the larger context for this passage, it becomes clear that "bad fruit" is not stressed out people who feel marginalized from society. Rather, according to Jesus' words in context, bad fruit is "everyone who hears these words of mine and does not do them" (v. 26 ESV). And "good fruit" is "everyone then who hears these words of mine and does them" (v. 24 ESV). In other words, *good fruit is characterized by obedience to Christ and to God's commands*. And bad fruit is sin.

The reality is that there are many issues of orthodox teaching that can cause considerable hardship in people's lives. Can you imagine the amount of distress and anger that would be caused if people followed the biblical guidelines on marriage and divorce (Matthew 19:3–12; 1 Corinthians 7)? Millions of Christians would experience angst, stress, depression, and frustration over what they believe are unreasonable demands to remain married to someone with whom they've fallen out of love. Sure, many people choose not to follow this teaching. But do we have the authority to change biblical teaching because it is difficult to live? It is hard to imagine Jesus and Paul adopting such an approach. In fact, by Vines's interpretation, the preaching of the apostles, which led them to be threatened, beaten, thrown in prison, and even killed, would be considered "bad fruit." And so would Paul's "thorn in the flesh." Even though Paul pleaded with Christ to remove it, he was told, "My grace is sufficient for you, for my power is made perfect in weakness" (2 Corinthians 12:9 ESV). For the sake of Christ, Paul willingly embraced "weaknesses, insults, hardships, persecutions, and calamities" (v. 10 ESV). Should we expect any less?

In a review of *God and the Gay Christian*, Christopher Yuan provides a proper context for experience and the interpretation of scripture:

> *A high view of Scripture is more than just talking about Scripture. It is learning from Scripture. Vines certainly talks about Scripture, but he tends to emphasize his experience and tangential background information, downplaying Scripture and its relevant literary and historical context.*
>
> *Experiences do inform our interpretation of Scripture. As a racial minority, biblical texts on sojourners and aliens mean more to me than to someone who is not a racial minority. However, experiences can also hinder the interpretation of Scripture. Although it is impossible to completely distance the*

interpretive process from one's experiences, it is important to recognize our biases and do our best to minimize them. A high view of Scripture involves measuring our experience against the Bible, not the other way around.

It appears to me that Vines starts with the conclusion that God blesses same-sex relationships and then moves backwards to find evidence. This is not exegesis, but a classic example of eisegesis (reading our own biases into a text). Like Vines, I also came out as a gay man while I was a student. I was a graduate student pursuing a doctorate in dentistry. Unlike Vines, I was not raised in a Christian home. Interestingly, a chaplain gave me a book from a gay-affirming author, John Boswell, claiming that homosexuality is not a sin. Like Vines, I was looking for biblical justification and wanted to prove that the Bible blesses gay relationships. As I read Boswell's book, the Bible was open next to it, and his assertions did not line up with Scripture. Eventually, I realized that I was wrong—that same-sex romantic relationships are a sin. My years of biblical language study in Bible college and seminary, and doctoral research in sexuality, only strengthened this conclusion. No matter how hard I tried to find biblical justification and no matter whether my same-sex temptations went away or not, God's word did not change. Years later I found out that the gay-affirming chaplain also recognized his error.[7]

One of the best defenses against cultural tolerance is for you and your church to develop deep convictions about truth and God's Word. Truth—moral truth—is derived from the character and nature of God. It is universal and is right for all people in all times within all cultures. Though moral truth is objective and to be discovered in scripture, we are called on to experience God's truth, personalize it, and live it out in our everyday lives. There are many ideas of how to apply scriptural truth to our lives, but there are not 101 ways to interpret the biblical text. God has an intended meaning, and our task is to draw out the true meaning of what was written in his Word.

If you are unsure of where your pastor, youth worker, or other church teachers stand on these matters, talk to them. Share and discuss what you are discovering in this book. Does your church teach that the Bible is authoritative and inspired by God? Does your church teach that moral truth is from God and universally true for us all? If so, you are in unity as Christ's body. Then you become a living representative of Christ's love to the world around you.

Paul wrote to the church in Philippi with these instructions: "Is there any encouragement from belonging to Christ? Any comfort from his love? Any fellowship together in the Spirit? Are your hearts tender and compassionate? Then make me truly happy by agreeing wholeheartedly with each other, loving one another, and working together with one mind and purpose" (Philippians 2:1–2).

Work with the leadership of your church and solicit their support as you attempt to set a generation free to know truth and love as God designed. In the next chapter—the final one of this book—we will offer you three suggestions to help you accomplish this within your church.

CHAPTER 12

YOU CAN MAKE A DIFFERENCE

The voice coming through the phone was familiar, but the question took me (Sean) by complete surprise. "You teach your students to defend their faith, right? Tell me, how do you know Christianity is true?" John and I had a special relationship that has lasted for more than a decade. But this was the first time he had shown any real interest in spiritual matters. Not only did he want to talk about God, but he wanted solid reasons to believe—he wanted proof and evidence before he would consider that Christ was really "the way, the truth, and the life" (John 14:6). John later told me his interest in God had been piqued when his cousin was diagnosed with a serious medical condition as a young teenager. His cousin recovered, but as John explained it, this experience "woke him up to his own mortality."

A few weeks after our phone conversation, John was heading back to college, so we decided to meet for a chat over coffee. As we sat down at the local coffee shop, John jumped right in. "I'm scientifically minded, so I need some evidence for the existence of God and the accuracy of the Bible. What can you show me?" For the next hour and a half we discussed some of the standard evidences for the existence of God, the death and resurrection of Jesus, and the reliability of the Bible. I did my best to answer his questions, trying to show that Christianity is rationally compelling and provides the most satisfying solution to the deepest longing of the heart. John didn't become a Christian at that point, but he confessed that he was very close and just needed more time to weigh the cost of his decision.

Our interaction with thousands of young people and the various studies conducted among youth convince us that our young people today, like John, are looking for answers. Many of them intuitively sense there is a truth out there, apart from themselves, which offers deeper solutions than what the culture has led them to believe. They may have bought into the cultural line because it is appealing. Who wouldn't want to think we can create any truth that validates whatever we want to do? And who wouldn't want a philosophy that prevents others from arousing our consciences by judging those choices? Being our own gods is a heady experience.

The problem is, self-determined morality may feel good for a while, but eventually most young people begin to sense that they are somehow out of alignment with reality. The wheels begin to wobble and they begin to veer into other lanes, causing damage to themselves and others. At that point, many begin to sense that there is something outside themselves that provides answers. The good news is that we have a message that God is there, and he offers a way they can live the life of joy he designed them to live.

Quite naturally, our young people—as well as ourselves—are looking for a belief that is relationally relevant. But created in God's image as we are, we equally want what is *evidentially credible*. I (Josh) have often said, "The head cannot rejoice in what the mind rejects." This generation is powerfully attracted to any message that is both *credible* and *relevant*. And the Bible is the ultimate repository of those two values.

As parents, pastors, youth workers, and Christian educators, we have a great opportunity and privilege to offer real answers that are credible and relevant. Throughout these past eleven chapters we have tried to present the credible truth of Christ and his Word that is also relationally relevant.

In this last chapter we want to reinforce that message and encourage you to be diligent in the following three areas:

1. Continually Develop Deepened Community

Building coalitions and connecting with other concerned parents and Christian leaders and educators is a good thing. Yet it will not replace the spiritual and relational nurture and strength derived from fellowship with an entire body of believers.

Jesus said, "Love each other. Just as I have loved you, you should love each other. Your love for one another will prove to the world that you are my disciples" (John 13:34–35). Genuine and mature Christian community is powerful and winsome. As our young people and the world around us hear and see us lovingly share our lives with one another, they will want what we have.

Why is it so important to have such a community of believers who know how to love and form deepened friendships? The following example makes the answer abundantly clear.

Wesley Hill is one of the most outspoken voices for the importance and role of celibacy within the Christian church. In his book *Washed and Waiting*, he writes openly and honestly about his personal journey as a gay man growing up in the evangelical world.

In a public discussion about homosexuality and the church at Biola University, Hill mentioned that many people with same-sex attraction are told there is no biblical justification for getting married to someone of the same sex and that celibacy is the only option. While he agrees with this, Hill did point out that celibacy often has negative connotations in the church because we have lost the art of friendship. The church has often focused solely on marriage at the expense of meaningful relationships in the larger body of Christ. While marriage is critical for the church and society, we must also build loving, committed relational communities that fully represent the entire body of Christ, including those who choose celibacy. We must recapture the biblical role of friendship, which Hill discusses in his book *Spiritual Friendship: Finding Love in the Church as a Celibate Gay Christian*. This is the kind of love that will draw our unbelieving world and provide the context for our young people to understand true tolerance.

2. Consistently Speak the Truth in Love

The underlying theme we have repeatedly emphasized throughout these pages is that moral truths come from the loving heart of a God who is motivated to provide for us and to protect us. Moral truth was never meant to be spoken or understood outside of a loving relationship. Being like Christ and speaking the truth in love are synonymous.

We must consistently speak the truth in love until it becomes a way of life. Doing so will equip us emotionally and relationally to help our young people counter cultural tolerance. Our young people need to see us as models of what moral truth looks like within relationships.

Your children are growing up in a culture that says they can tell if something is true by whether or not it works. They want to see things work before they accept them. This gives you an opportunity to be a working model of what truth looks like in the context of relationships. You don't have to be a perfect model, but you can be an authentic one. Your young people know you are not perfect, but they do want authenticity. So it's important that you be real, warts and all, and share with them the truth that is the ultimate in authenticity. That will show them that Christlikeness not only works, but it is also attractive. And that will draw them to emulate it.

3. Build Relationships with People of a Different Mind-Set

How can we Christians change the perception that we are hateful, bigoted, and intolerant? There is one vital step each one of us can take—build genuine relationships with people who see the world very differently than we do. We will overcome the cultural perception that Christians are intolerant bigots only when people hear this claim and their first thought is, *That doesn't seem right. I know Christians, and they're loving, gracious, and thoughtful.* Each one of us has a responsibility to build real relationships with people who reject our most cherished beliefs. It is easy to build relationships with people who are like us. How many of us are willing to do it with people who are *un*like us?

Not too long ago, I (Sean) had one of the most interesting and memorable evenings I had had in years. For two and a half hours, I had a dialogue with fourteen skeptics, atheists, and agnostics from a freethought organization based in Southern California, close to where I live.

How did this come about? The idea for this conversation came from a book I cowrote on the New Atheism.[1] The purpose of the book is to give readers the tools necessary to respond to the toughest questions raised by the New Atheists but without the typical rancor and divisiveness that so often characterizes such exchanges. Our goal in the book was to take atheists' objections seriously but to respond with "gentleness and respect," as Peter counsels (1 Peter 3:15 NIV). We hoped to answer their critiques while modeling *how* to engage nonbelievers lovingly.

Since Christians seem to be the primary readers of Christian books, I wondered how I could get non-Christians to seriously entertain the arguments of the book. How could I *really* reach out to atheists? After all, that was one of the main reasons we wrote it. Then the idea hit me. The book is about personally engaging skeptics, so why don't I put the message into practice and actually try to converse with atheists? So I e-mailed my idea to Bruce, the leader of the freethought group, wondering if he would share my enthusiasm. To my pleasant surprise, he loved the idea!

Bruce began the evening by expressing his amazement that I would come to such an event. From his perspective, few Christians are willing to voluntarily sit on the "hot seat" with a group of skeptics. He may be right. While I appreciated the compliment, it actually saddened me: Why aren't Christians regularly going to skeptics' meetings? Why aren't we building relationships with nonbelievers? What are we afraid of?

Some of the questions the skeptics asked were predictable while others caught me off guard. They ranged from my views on stem cell research to separation of church and state. We also talked about the common ground shared by atheists and Christians. They were very cordial, respectful, and quite interested in what I had to say. Bruce even began the evening by giving me permission *not* to answer any question that made me feel uncomfortable. While I passed on the offer, it was a very gracious gesture.

After doing my best to answer their questions, I turned the tables and asked some questions of my own. Rather than trying to "nail" them with tough apologetic questions (as some of my friends suggested), I wanted to build common ground and try to understand how they perceive Christians. I asked questions such as, "How can Christians improve their interactions with skeptics?" and "What bad impressions do Christians leave?" Their answers were eye-opening. They included the following:

- "Hypocrisy. Christians often focus on particular sins,

such as homosexuality, while they are committing other egregious sins in their own lives." (The young man who shared this mentioned that some of his Christian friends regularly get drunk but also frequently condemn homosexuality as immoral.)

- "Christians don't take their religion seriously. Why don't they read, study, and follow the Bible if they really believe it is a word from the almighty God?"
- "Christians often criticize me for not having good reasons for what I believe, but when pressed, they can't provide evidence for their beliefs either. They should at least be consistent and admit this."
- "Stop making slanderous remarks about non-Christians. I grew up in church and heard more cheap shots made at atheists than any other group."

I listened to their concerns and did my best to articulate the Christian position as clearly and graciously as I could. My goal was not to persuade them that Christianity is true in the course of the evening, but "to put a stone in their shoe," as apologist Greg Koukl often says.[2] In fact, rather than defining success as persuading them on any particular issue, I hoped to show them that Christians are thoughtful, compassionate, and likable. I also brought them a free signed copy of my book and was hoping they might read it with an open heart and mind.

The highlight of the evening came toward the end. Bruce had intentionally set aside some time for us to share our grievances with each other. He began by asking me to share my grievances with atheists. In other words, what are my problems and frustrations with atheists? I could tell he had a few gripes against Christians that he was anxious to share! But instead of taking the bait, I shared about my atheist friends and family members whom I dearly love. Rather than lumping all atheists into a group and stereotyping them, I told them that I loved atheists. That's right, I had the opportunity to share my love for atheists with a group of skeptics *on their own turf*. And I meant it. Then I said, "My problem is not with atheists but with atheism. It's a false worldview."

I don't share this to give myself a pat on the back. It's not about *me*. It's about Christians learning to love people with the same love with which Christ loved us. We can no longer maintain a fortress mentality—we *must* get out of our comfort zones and truly engage different people with the love of Christ. Here is the bottom line: If we want to overcome the perception that Christians are hateful bigots, we must each be willing to build genuine, loving relationships with people around us and show them otherwise. We must humbly approach people, not as opponents, but with eagerness to listen to and learn from them as fellow human beings and a willingness to love them despite our differences.

In 1995 Laura McCorvey, the "Jane Roe" of the famous *Roe v. Wade* Supreme Court case of 1973, shocked the nation by converting to Christianity, getting baptized, and joining the pro-life movement. Most powerfully, it was the director of the pro-life group Operation Rescue who influenced her. According to McCorvey, her worldview began to change when the director stopped treating her like an antagonist and simply loved her as a human being. Thus, while proclaiming truth is necessary for transformation, love and grace are what soften the heart.

4. Consistently Take Advantage of Resources

I (Josh) remember vividly when I held my firstborn child in my arms. As I looked at little Kelly, my knees went weak. It dawned on me that now I was a father, but I didn't have a clue about fathering.

To correct that deficiency, I sought wisdom from some good role models on fathering and gathered as many good resources as I could find. Raising children in today's world isn't easy. Neither is being an effective youth worker or a capable pastor to today's families. It is an uphill battle. Take advantage of the experience of others. Tap into resources from those who have insights into our culture, who understand where our young people are, and who offer biblically based solutions.

Here are a few recommendations for helping youth develop a Christian worldview:

1. Summit Ministries. Summit offers two-week student conferences to help sixteen- to twenty-two-year-olds develop a biblical worldview. They bring in world-class speakers to help students develop convictions about the reliability of the Bible, the validity of being pro-life, and the legitimacy of a biblical view of sexuality, as well as about God and politics, intelligent design, and more. Conferences are held in Tennessee and Colorado, and I (Sean) personally host a conference in Southern California each June (www.summit.org).

2. As for apologetics resources, we recommend Stand to Reason, a ministry that has a popular radio show, books, and articles, and hosts student conferences nationwide (www.str.org); Reasonable Faith, the ministry of philosopher William Lane Craig (www.reasonablefaith.org); and Cold Case Christianity

(www.coldcasechristianity.com), the ministry of our friend J. Warner Wallace.

3. Biola University offers an MA in apologetics that is distance-based for working professionals. If you have ever thought about studying apologetics formally, we certainly recommend Biola. They also host multiple conferences across the nation each year.[3]

4. You also might consider holding a group study of this book. A group study guide is available at www.barbourbooks.com/SG2. You can either introduce this book and its study guide to the church small group you are a part of or form your own group. Both of us have additional books and group courses you can tap into as well. Visit www.josh.org and www.seanmcdowell.org and click on Resources.

As an added resource, for a limited time we (Josh and Sean) are teaming up to give our young people and their parents answers through live events. We will be conducting a Friday night and all day Saturday event called the "Heroic Truth Experience." We want to help your children realize that God has given us a reliable and trusted Bible. We will dig deep into the questions young people are facing in a skeptical and anti-Christian culture. We will cover questions about God, creation, how you can know what is true, and a host of issues designed to equip your children to "always be prepared to give an answer to everyone who asks you to give a reason for the hope that you have" (1 Peter 3:15 NIV). We must not allow the world to confuse our young people with false reasoning and lure them out of their faith. For more details about these events, go to www.heroictruth.com.

You can make a difference in your family and community as you continually develop deepened community within the body of Christ, consistently speak the truth in love, build genuine relationships with nonbelievers, and constantly take advantage of biblically based resources. Setting a generation free to know truth and love as God designed is a day to day, month after month, year after year process. And remember—there are no quick fixes, magic bullets, or guarantees when it comes to influencing the next generation. We are called to patience, long-suffering, and even allowing adult children to make their own choices while we labor and pray for them fervently. True tolerance involves loving people and suffering while they do something we think is absolutely wrong, which is exactly what Christ does for us. Whether or not young people respond to our love, there is something beautiful about responding as Christ did—even if our culture considers such love *in*tolerance.

NOTES

CHAPTER 1

1. Mark Regnerus, "The Mission Creep of Dignity," The Witherspoon Institute, January 12, 2015, http://thepublicdiscourse.com/2015/01/14253.

2. Brad Stetson and Joseph G. Conti, *The Truth about Tolerance: Pluralism, Diversity and the Culture Wars* (Downers Grove, IL: InterVarsity, 2005), 12.

3. "Teens Look to Parents More Than Friends for Sexual Role Models," Science Daily, June 15, 2011, http://sciencedaily.com/releases/2011/06/110615120355.htm.

4. "Learn How to Engage Millennials," Barna Group, November 2014, e-mail from barna@barna.org.

5. Jeffrey Rosenberg and W. Bradford Wilcox, "The Importance of Fathers in the Healthy Development of Children," U.S. Department of Health and Human Services, 2006, http://childwelfare.gov/pubs/usermanuals/father-hood/fatherhood.pdf.

6. "Talking to Your Teen about Sexuality," University of Florida/IFAS Extension, Hillsborough County, http://hillsborough.ifas.ufl.edu/documents/pdf/fcs/A-Z_family/sexuality.pdf.

CHAPTER 2

1. David Kinnaman and Gabe Lyons, *unChristian: What a New Generation Really Thinks about Christianity. . .and Why It Matters* (Grand Rapids: Baker, 2007), 92–93.

2. Ibid.

3. Todd Starnes, "City Threatens to Arrest Ministers Who

Refuse to Perform Same-Sex Marriages," FoxNews.com, October 20, 2014, http://www.foxnews.com/opinion/2014/10/20/city-threatens-to-arrest-ministers-who-refuse-to-perform-same-sex-weddings/.

4. Samuel Smith, "Marquette University Suspends Tenured Professor after He Criticized Instructor Who Prohibited Student from Discussing Gay Marriage Opposition," Christian Post, December 19, 2014, http://www.christianpost.com/news/marquette-university-suspends-tenured-professor-after-he-criticized-instructor-who-prohibited-student-from-discussing-gay-marriage-opposition-131458/.

5. Webster's New World Dictionary of American English, 3rd ed., s.v. "tolerate."

6. Thomas A. Helmbock, "Insights on Tolerance," Cross and Crescent (publication of Lambda Chi Alpha International Fraternity), summer 1996, 2.

7. "Americans Are Most Likely to Base Truth on Feelings," Barna Group, February 12, 2002, https://www.barna.org/barna-update/article/5-barna-update/67-americans-are-most-likely-to-base-truth-on-feelings#.VNPoYu85Cpo.

8. "Barna Survey Examines Changes in Worldview among Christians over the Past 13 Years," Barna Group, March 6, 2009, https://www.barna.org/barna-update/21-transformation/252-barna-survey-examines-changes-in-worldview-among-christians-over-the-past-13-years#.VOdMxCmaAnU.

9. Jacob Poushter, "What's Morally Acceptable? It Depends on Where in the World You Live," PewResearchCenter, April 15, 2014, http://www.pewresearch.org/fact-tank/2014/04/15/whats-morally-acceptable-it-depends-on-where-in-the-world-you-live/.

10. Ibid.

11. California legislators' letter cited in Olga R. Rodriguez, "San Francisco Archbishop Tells Teachers to Abide by Anti-Gay Morality Clause," TPM News, February 18, 2015, http://talkingpointsmemo.com/news/california-lawmakers-archbishop-morality-clauses.

CHAPTER 3

1. Andrew Walker, "The Atlanta Fire Chief Fired," First Things, January 14, 2015, http://www.firstthings.com/blogs/firstthoughts/2015/01/the-atlanta-fire-chief-fired.

2. The Editorial Board, "God, Gays and the Atlanta Fire Department," *New York Times*, January 13, 2015, http://www.nytimes.com/2015/01/13/opinion/god-gays-and-the-atlanta-fire-department.html?partn.

3. Walker, "Atlanta Fire Chief Fired."

4. https://www.washingtonpost.com/posteverything/wp/2015/05/12/im-a-florist-but-i-refused-to-do-flowers-for-my-gay-friends-wedding/.

5. *Merriam-Webster's Collegiate Dictionary*, 10th ed., s.v. "truth."

6. Brad Stetson and Joseph G. Conti, *The Truth about Tolerance: Pluralism, Diversity and the Culture Wars* (Downers Grove, IL: InterVarsity, 2005), 43.

7. J. P. Moreland, *Kingdom Triangle: Recover the Christian Mind, Renovate the Soul, Restore the Spirit's Power* (Grand Rapids: Zondervan, 2007), 77.

8. William Lane Craig, "God Is Not Dead Yet," July 3, 2008, *Christianity Today* 52, no. 7 (July 3, 2008): 22, http://www.christianitytoday.com/ct/2008/july/13.22.html?start=6.

9. Joel Achenbach, "Why Do Many Reasonable People Doubt Science?" *National Geographic*, March 2015, http://ngm.nationalgeographic.com/2015/03/science-doubters/achenbach-text.

CHAPTER 4

1. Samantha, "Confessions of a Half-Virgin," *HuffPost Teen*, December 9, 2014; updated December 10, 2014, http://www.huffingtonpost.com/2014/12/09/why-i-consider-myself-hal_n_6297134.html.

2. Ibid.

3. Alexa Tsoulis-Reay, "What It's Like to Date a Horse," *New York*, November 20, 2014, http://nymag.com/scienceofus/2014/11/what-its-like-to-date-a-horse.html. We do not recommend that you read this article as it is disturbing. We simply provide the documentation as support for our point.

4. Napp Nazworth, "Christians Who Cave to the 'New Tolerance' Only Make Matters Worse, Mary Eberstadt Says," *Christian Post*, November 17, 2014, http://www.christianpost.com/news/christians-who-cave-to-the-new-intolerance-only-make-it-worse-mary-eberstadt-says-129778/.

5. Leonardo Blair, "Former Megachurch Pastor Rob Bell Tells Oprah the Church Is 'Moments Away' from Embracing Gay Marriage," *Christian Post*, February 17, 2015, http://www.christianpost.com/news/former-megachurch-pastor-rob-bell-tells-oprah-the-church-is-moments-away-from-embracing-gay-marriage-134264/.

6. See James Kirkup, "Muslims Must Embrace Our British Values, David Cameron Says," *Telegraph*, February 5, 2011, http://www.telegraph.co.uk/news/politics/david-cameron/8305346/Muslims-must-embrace-our-British-values-David-Cameron-says.html.

7. Brad Stetson and Joseph G. Conti, *The Truth about Tolerance: Pluralism, Diversity and the Culture Wars* (Downers Grove, IL: InterVarsity, 2005), 83.

8. Friedrich Nietzsche, ed. and trans. Walter Kaufman, trans. R. J. Hollingdale, *The Will to Power* (New York: Vintage, 1968), 401.

9. Luc Ferry, *A Brief History of Thought: A Philosophical Guide to Living* (New York: Harper Perennial, 2011), 72.

10. Greg Gilman, "Jesse Ventura Vents More 'American Sniper' Criticism by Comparing US to Nazis, Communists: 'We Behave the Same Way Now,' " *The Wrap*, February 4, 2015, http://thewrap.com/jesse-ventura-vents-more-american-sniper-criticism-by-comparing-us-to-nazis-communists-we-behave-the-same-way-now/.

11. Frank Turek, *Stealing from God: Why Atheists Need to Make Their Case* (Colorado Springs: Navpress 2014), 97.

12. Christopher Hitchens, *God Is Not Great: How Religion Poisons Everything* (New York: Twelve Books, 2007), 13.

13. Friedrich Nietzsche, *The Antichrist*, intro. by H. L. Mencken (Torrance, CA: Noontide, 1980), 180.

14. See Sean McDowell and Jonathan Morrow, *Is God Just a Human Invention? And Seventeen Other Questions Raised by the New Atheists* (Grand Rapids: Kregel, 2010), 151–52.

CHAPTER 5

1. A. W. Tozer, *Tozer Speaks: Volume One: 128 Compelling & Authoritative Teachings of A. W. Tozer* (Chicago: Wingspread, 2010).

2. For evidence to back up this claim, see Josh McDowell, *The Bare Facts: 39 Questions Your Parents Hope You Never Ask about Sex* (Chicago: Moody, 2011).

3. Drawn from Josh and Sean McDowell, *The Unshakable Truth: How You Can Experience the 12 Essentials of a Relevant Faith* (Eugene, OR: Harvest House, 2010), 115–16.

CHAPTER 6

1. Simon LeVay, "A Difference in Hypothalamic Structure between Heterosexual and Homosexual Men," *Science* 253, no. 5023 (1991): 1034–37.

2. Dean Hamer et al., "A Linkage between DNA Markers on the X Chromosome and Male Sexual Orientation," *Science* 261, (1993): 321–27.

3. Simon LeVay quoted in David Nimmons, "Sex and the Brain—Neurobiologist Simon LeVay Found a Link between Brain Structure and Homosexuality," *Discover*, March 1994, 64.

4. Dean Hamer and Peter Copeland, *Living with Our Genes: Why They Matter More Than You Think* (New York: Bantam Doubleday Dell, 1998), 188.

5. Dean Hamer quoted in Anastasia Toufexis, "New Evidence of a 'Gay Gene,' " *Time* 146, no. 20 (1995): 95.

6. American Psychological Association, "Answers to Your Questions: For a Better Understanding of Sexual Orientation & Homosexuality" brochure (Washington, DC: American Psychological Association, 2008).

7. Susan Donaldson James, "Thrill-Seeking Gene May Lead to Promiscuous Sex, Cheating," ABC News, December 6, 2010, http://abcnews.go.com/Health/scientists-discover-gene-responsible-cheating-promiscuous-sex-habits/story?id=12322891.

CHAPTER 7

1. Thanks to Amy Hall for drawing this example to our attention. See Justin Taylor, "What Are We Apart from Christ?" *Gospel Coalition*, August 27, 2010, http://www.thegospelcoalition.org/blogs/justintaylor/2010/08/27/what-are-we-apart-from-christ/.

2. Adapted from Sean McDowell and John Stonestreet, *Same-Sex Marriage: A Thoughtful Approach to God's Design for Marriage* (Grand Rapids: Baker, 2014), 40–41.

3. To find out more about The Reformation Project, go to http://www.reformationproject.org/.

CHAPTER 8

1. Duke Pesta, "Moral Relativism and the Crisis of Contemporary Education," The New American.com, December 1, 2011, http://www.thenewamerican.com/culture/education/item/372-moral-relativism-and-the-crisis-of-contemporary-education.

2. Justin P. McBrayer, "Why Our Children Don't Think There Are Moral Facts," *New York Times*, March 2, 2015, http://opinionator.blogs.nytimes.com/2015/03/02/why-our-children-dont-think-there-are-moral-facts/?_r=2.

3. Todd Starnes, "Teacher Tells Student He Can't Read the Bible in Classroom," Fox News.com, May 5, 2014, http://www.foxnews.com/opinion/2014/05/05/teacher-tells-student-cant-read-bible-in-my-classroom/.

4. Ibid.

5. Ken Klukowski, "School Employee Tells Five-Year-Old She Can't Pray for Lunch," *Breitbart News*, April 2, 2014, http://www.breitbart.com/big-government/2014/04/02/school-worker-tells-5-year-old-she-can-t-pray-for-lunch/.

6. Todd Starnes, "School Tells Child She Can't Write about God," Fox News.com, September 11, 2013, http://radio.foxnews.com/toddstarnes/top-stories/school-tells-child-she-cant-write-about-god.html.

7. Todd Starnes, "School Tells Kids: Stop Praying to Jesus,

Singing Amazing Grace," Fox News.com, November 10, 2014, http://www.foxnews.com/opinion/2014/11/10/school-tells-kids-stop-praying-to-jesus-singing-amazing-grace/.

8. Tyler Kingkade, "'Stomp on Jesus' Controversy at Florida Atlantic University Draws Gov. Rick Scott's Involvement," *HuffPost*, March 27, 2013, http://www.huffingtonpost.com/2013/03/27/stomp-on-jesus_n_2963400.html.

9. Ibid.

CHAPTER 9

1. "Wedding Venue Appeals Ruling," *Akron* [Ohio] *Beacon Journal*, November 12, 2014, B12.

2. Curtis M. Wong, "Masterpiece Cakeshop's Jack Phillips Vows to Stop Making Wedding Cakes Altogether after Court Rules in Favor of Gay Couple," *HuffPost*, June 3, 2014, http://www.huffingtonpost.com/2014/06/03/jack-phillips-masterpiece-cakeshop-_n_5438726.html.

3. Ibid., 115–21.

4. C. S. Lewis, *Mere Christianity* (New York: Collier, 1960), 118.

CHAPTER 10

1. Illustration adapted from Josh McDowell, *10 Commitments for Dads* (Eugene, OR: Harvest House, 2014), chap. 9.

2. Content of this chapter was adapted in part from the Right from Wrong resources of Josh McDowell and Bob Hostetler, *Right from Wrong: What You Need to Know to Help Youth Make Right Choices* (Thomas Nelson, 1994) and Truth Slayers series (Thomas Nelson, 1995).

CHAPTER 11

1. Masuma Ahoja, "Teens Are Spending More Time Consuming Media, on Mobile Devices," Washington Post Live, March 13, 2013, http://www.washingtonpost.com/postlive/teens-are-spending-more-time-consuming-media-on-mobile-devices/2013/03/12/309bb242-8689-11e2-98a3-b3db6b9ac586_story.html.

2. Kim Parker, "Modern Parenthood: Roles of Moms and Dads Converge as They Balance Work and Family," PewResearchCenter, March 14, 2013, http://www.pewsocialtrends.org/2013/03/14/modern-parenthood-roles-of-moms-and-dads-converge-as-they-balance-work-and-family/.

3. Ibid.

4. Matthew Vines, *God and the Gay Christian* (New York: Convergent, 2014), 2.

5. Ibid., 13–14.

6. Ibid, 14.

7. Christopher Yuan, "Why 'God and the Gay Christian' Is Wrong about the Bible and Same-Sex Relationships," *Christianity Today*, June 9, 2014, http://www.christianitytoday.com/ct/2014/june-web-only/why-matthew-vines-is-wrong-about-bible-same-sex-relationshi.html.

CHAPTER 12

1. Sean McDowell and Jonathan Morrow, *Is God Just a Human Invention? And Seventeen Other Questions Raised by the New Atheists* (Grand Rapids: Kregel, 2010).

2. Gregory Koukl, *Tactics: A Game Plan for Discussing Your Christian Convictions* (Grand Rapids: Zondervan, 2009), 38.

3. See Biola University, http://www.biola.edu/academics/sas/apologetics/.

ABOUT THE AUTHORS

Josh McDowell has been at the forefront of cultural trends and groundbreaking ministry for more than five decades. He shares the essentials of the Christian faith in everyday language to help youth, families, churches, leaders, and individuals of all ages be prepared for the life of faith and the work of the ministry. Since 1961 Josh has delivered more than 27,000 talks to more than 25 million people in 125 countries. He is the author or coauthor of 142 books, including *More Than a Carpenter* and *New Evidence That Demands a Verdict*, recognized by *World* magazine as one of the top forty books of the twentieth century. Josh's books are available in more than one hundred different languages. Josh and his wife Dottie are quick to acknowledge that after their love for the Lord, family is their greatest joy and top priority. They have been married for over forty-five years and have four wonderful children and ten beloved grandchildren. For more information, please visit www.josh.org.

Sean McDowell, PhD, is an assistant professor at Biola University in the MA Christian apologetics program. He is also a bestselling author of over fifteen books. Sean is an internationally recognized speaker for conferences, universities, schools, and churches. He and his wife Stephanie and their three children live in Southern California.

**Please enjoy the following sample from
Josh McDowell's book**

CHAPTER
1

WHAT'S IN A WORD?

Nineteen years old and quite a skeptic. That described me as I left college and traveled to Europe to do research in an attempt to disprove Christianity—specifically to show that the Bible was historically unreliable and that Jesus was by no means the Son of God.

Standing in the Glasgow University library in Scotland, I stared at an ancient New Testament manuscript. It was a fragment from John 16, and the ink and papery substance on which it was written were more than sixteen hundred years old. This rare, third-century, handwritten portion of the Gospel of John was housed under a protective glass case in the university library. It was a priceless artifact that quoted the words of Jesus.

As I stood there, a strange and unexpected feeling washed over me. Though I could not read or understand a single line of the Greek in which that manuscript was written, those words seemed to reach out to me in an almost mystical way. Even though I was an unbeliever at the time, I sensed an uncanny power about those words.

TODAY'S NOISY WORDS

Words. The right ones used in the right way can be powerful. But in today's world, I'm afraid a lot of people use a lot of words to produce merely a lot of noise.

Everywhere you look, you see people using a barrage of words in bite-size chunks in hopes of communicating. Take texting, for example. Our generation is "connected" now more than ever by smartphones. According to a recent Experian Marketing Services digital marketer report, the average number of texts per month by eighteen- to twenty-four-year-olds is 3,853. That is more than 128 texts a day.[1]

People are using words at an unprecedented rate through Facebook as well. Within the first quarter of 2014, Facebook reported more than 1.15 billion active users per month.[2] The market research company eMarketer estimates that 40 percent of all US children under the age of twelve are online monthly. Nearly half will be online by 2015.[3]

It's clear in today's world of texts, Twitter, Facebook, and e-mails that we are transmitting words at record levels. But are all these words truly *connecting* us, or are many of them simply a lot of noise? The Creator of words had a purpose in mind when he gave us the ability to write words and speak them to others. Used properly, words can effectively connect us relationally. Words are important, and the God-breathed words of scripture are the most important of all. But we must *listen* to how words are being used in order to understand their true meaning.

LISTENING FOR THE MEANING OF WORDS

We humans have the unique ability to make varied sounds and arrange them in specific combinations that we call words. And each of these words is designed to mean something in particular. The languages we speak are composed of words, which are the building blocks of thoughts, ideas, and expressed feelings. When we assemble words in sentences to represent our thoughts, ideas, and feelings, they become the basic elements of our human communication.

Using words enables us to accomplish much of what we do in life. Through words we can communicate how to get from one place to another, complete tasks, form friendships, express love to a spouse, raise a family, and express our views on countless subjects. Words can transmit creative thoughts and ingenious ideas, but their most meaningful purpose is when we use them to connect to one another relationally. Yet when we're not attentive to words, or we fail to listen carefully to what someone says, words can become mere sounds or marks on a page and lose their power to connect us.

I remember the tragic beginning of my honeymoon. Dottie and I had known each other for only six short months before we married. I figured my lovely wife and I had a lifetime to really get to know each other, so I was in no particular hurry to discover all there was to know about her. But that wasn't the case for my new bride. I soon discovered that she was anxious to share her entire life story with me on our honeymoon.

We were driving a long distance through Mexico to Acapulco when Dottie began to tell me about herself, her family, her childhood, her likes and dislikes, her views on politics, marriage, and child rearing. You name it, and Dottie was prepared to talk about it.

I remember that, at some point, my receptive facilities went into overload and all the words she was saying began to sound like mere noise. Meanwhile, I was also trying to interpret the confusing road signs and stopping occasionally to fumble with a stack of maps. After a while, Dottie's talking became intermittent, and eventually she became silent. During that whole time, I had said little except the occasional "Yeah," "Uh-huh," and "I see." But to be honest, I got practically nothing out of my new wife's marathon of words. In fact, I hardly even noticed when she stopped talking.

Dottie had used a lot of words, but they meant little to me and did nothing to bring us closer together. Of course, she hadn't felt the need to explain to me what should have been obvious—that her exercise in self-disclosure was simply so that her brand-new husband could better know his brand-new wife. But when it became clear that I was clueless to what she was trying to accomplish, Dottie didn't remain shut down for long. She blew up!

It wasn't the best start to a honeymoon, but after Dottie explained what she was trying to do, and I did a lot of apologizing, we figured it out together. From that point on, our words began to make sense to one another. I began to see the loving heart of my wife, who wanted me to know her for who she is, and she began to see a husband who, despite his initial lapse into insensitivity, wanted to make his new wife happy.

As Dottie and I look back at our honeymoon now, we laugh about it. But it taught us the importance of words and of listening and interpreting and finding the true meaning of thoughts and feelings that flow from our hearts.

It takes time and effort to communicate effectively with meaningful words. It also takes time and effort to listen, translate, and accurately interpret the meaning of those words. In a real sense, there is an art to using words. And the God-breathed words of scripture, in particular, artfully communicate a powerful message designed to bring meaning to our lives.

GOD IS THE MASTER OF POWERFUL WORDS

"God said, 'Let there be. . .'" (Genesis 1:3). At some point in the distant past, God spoke words. And when he did, things happened. There was such creative power behind those words that the sun, stars, and moon burst into being. Out of God's mouth came words that formed everything that exists, including you and me.

Not only did God use powerful words to bring about the existence of all things, he also used words to bring meaning to our lives and our relationships. Then, in time, he had those meaningful words committed to writing.

The Bible, God-breathed words of life, is meant to give us everything we need in order to understand who we are, why we're here, and where we're going. It is made up of living words from God himself to guide us to the very meaning of life, love, relationships, and the joy God originally intended for his children. The words in the Bible are extremely powerful. Yet, for whatever reason, far too many people in the world have failed to be gripped by the power of those words.

In the pages of *God-Breathed*, we want to journey together to recapture the awe, the mystery, the passion, and the power of God's words in his book. The Bible is no ordinary book. Within its pages are hidden the answers to our every need, direction for our lives, and practical insights for living a life of fulfillment and joy. That is not merely hype; it is what the Author of the book intended from the very beginning.

Consider the following true story about how the consummate master of words unveiled the meaning of scripture to those he loved.

It had been the worst week of their lives. The two travelers tried to sort things out as they walked the seven miles from the city of Jerusalem to the village of Emmaus. Their greatest hope for being freed from the oppression of the Roman Empire had been in a man they thought was their Messiah. But three days ago he had been taken by the Romans and crucified. Their hopes had died with the death of the one they called Jesus.

That's the way life tends to be. We hope for things, and some things even work out; but, more often than not, we face disappointments, heartache, and loss. Even though we try to find meaning and joy during troubled times, it's an ongoing struggle. That's how these two men may have felt as they walked together along the dusty road.

"I don't know what to think about it," the first one said.

"I don't either," the other replied. "I've heard that Peter himself saw the empty tomb."

"Yeah," his companion countered, "but that doesn't necessarily mean Jesus was raised from the dead like the women are claiming."

About that time, a stranger joined them on their journey. "What are you two talking about?" he asked.

One of the two, whose name was Cleopas, responded, "You must be the only person in Jerusalem who hasn't heard about all the things that have happened there the last few days" (Luke 24:18).

"What things?" the stranger asked.

The two companions told the uninformed stranger all about Jesus—who they had believed he was, how he'd been crucified, and how he was now reported to have risen from the dead. They may have shared their emotional ups and downs. They no doubt talked about the joy they had experienced with Jesus, the hope they had placed in him, and their disappointment in the fact that the Romans had killed him.

After hearing what the two travelers said, and sensing their confusion, the stranger began to quote the words of God to them. Drawing upon the writings of Moses and all the prophets, he explained to them what the scriptures said and meant about this Messiah whose name was Jesus.

When they arrived at their destination, the two men asked their new friend to join them for a meal and a night's stay. When they sat down to eat, the stranger broke the bread, blessed it, and handed it to them. Then something astonishing happened. The men recognized this stranger as none other than Jesus himself. And then he vanished before their very eyes. They turned to each other in amazement and said, "Didn't our hearts burn within us as he talked with us on the road and explained the scriptures to us?" (Luke 24:32).

These two companions had heard from childhood the words Jesus quoted to them from the scriptures. They had grown up reading these scriptures, but the master of powerful words breathed new life into them. And as he did, he inspired and warmed their hearts, transformed disappointment into hope, and gave them insights for living a life of joy. That is what God's Word is meant to do for us. "For the word of God is alive and powerful" (Hebrews 4:12). It reveals the true heart of a God who loves us and wants us to know him. God's Word has the power to draw us into an intimate relationship with him that will truly transform our lives.

GOD IS THE MASTER OF RELIABLE WORDS

As a nineteen-year-old university student, I was intrigued by the ancient writings of scripture. Though I was a skeptic, as I've mentioned, I sensed a strange power about the words I saw penned on that sixteen-hundred-year-old manuscript. But I didn't trust them to be reliable. In fact, I initially set out to prove that today's Bible is nothing more than a collection of distorted and unreliable records of historical and mythical events. I reasoned that if we couldn't trust that the writings of scripture had been accurately handed down over the centuries, we would have no basis for the truth claims of the Bible. Simply put, if the Bible is not a reliable document of history, then everything it says about God and the Christian faith is in question.

Have you ever wondered whether the ancient scribes who copied the scriptures left things out or added things in? Could God have given Moses *twelve* commandments only to have some scribe along the way decide to eliminate two of them? What if, during the copying of the Gospel of John, a hundred years after he wrote it, a scribe left out five chapters? Imagine if overzealous scribes added to or twisted the recorded things Jesus said or did in order to inject their own ideas. How can we be sure that we have a Bible that accurately represents what God inspired people to write on his behalf? Since we have none of the original manuscripts, how can we know that the copies in our possession are reliable and accurate?

Face it, if we can't be confident that scripture is a reliable book of history, we can't assert that it is the power-filled Word of God. Sure, God may be the master of powerful words, but if his words have not been passed down accurately to us, the power of those words would be lost.

Today, I am convinced beyond a reasonable doubt that scripture is reliable and its very words are God's own and have real power. As a university student, somewhere in the hidden recesses of my heart I wanted to believe God was real and cared for me. But I had no true basis for believing that, unless the Bible was reliable.

You don't either.

You may sincerely believe in God and that his Word has power.

Yet at some point, that faith will be tested. If your faith is rooted in evidence that the Bible is truly reliable, you will have all the assurance necessary to trust that God's Word is absolutely true. I can assure you, there is clear evidence that God has miraculously superintended the transmission and copying of his words to us, so that we can know we have his truth as he intended. You and I can know that God's Word has been handed down to us reliably; and because of that, we can experience his powerful words in our everyday lives. That is what this book is about: knowing with certainty that we can experience the power of God's Word as revealed in the Bible, because it's reliable.

WHAT TO EXPECT

Knowing that the Bible is a reliable conveyor of God's Word is a prerequisite to understanding that his words are powerful. So it would seem logical to discuss the Bible's reliability before dealing with its power. But I want to reverse the order, and here's why: Frankly, I want to appeal to an inner desire that I believe we all share. Somewhere deep inside, you no doubt find the idea appealing that there is an all-powerful being in the universe who loves you dearly. It speaks to a deep desire in every human heart. I want to appeal to that desire before I appeal to your intellect. That's why I want to start by sharing with you how and why God's book has power. My hope is that this groundwork will help you capture more deeply the beauty, mystery, and intrigue of God's Word. To truly sense the power of scripture is to be captivated by its Author and to develop a true love for him and a longing to know the deep meaning of the words he has recorded for you.

So in the next seven chapters, we will explore the power of scripture—how it is truly a living book; what its true purpose is; how it was meant to be interpreted; how it is relevant to your everyday life; and how you can gain a true love for this unique, one-of-a-kind document.

After we've been gripped by the power of the God-breathed Word, we will uncover how truly reliable it is, and we will develop a deepened trust that the words in the Bible have been accurately passed down to us. This is what gives us assurance that God has revealed his true nature to us. We will examine how scripture is reliable using modern tests for any book's reliability; we'll confront apparent contradictions in scripture; and we'll explain how the Bible can become more alive *to you*.

Warning! Be prepared to be captivated by God's Word. When we truly understand and experience the power and reliability of scripture, our "hearts will burn within us." This is because we are not simply talking about recorded history and stories of biblical characters. We are talking about a book that is strangely alive.

My prayer is that you will discover in the God-breathed words of Scripture a greater power and relevance to your own life. There is a mystery to God's book, and he wants you to discover it. There are treasures and insights you need in order to deal with the challenges of life. And God wants you to find them by looking for *him* in his Word. "'If you look for me wholeheartedly, you will find me. I will be found by you,' says the Lord" (Jeremiah 29:13–14).

Let's start looking!